100 BIBLICAL INSPIRATIONS

Simple Honest Plain Compelling Truths

Dr. Garfield E. Como
Judy A. Como

100 BIBLICAL INSPIRATIONS

Simple Honest Plain Compelling Truths

Copyright © 2018 by **Dr. Garfield E. Como & Judy A. Como**

ISBN: 978-1-944652-56-2

Printed in the United States of America. All rights reserved solely by the publisher. This book or parts thereof may not be reproduced in any form, stored in a retrieval system, or transmitted in any form by any means - electronic, mechanical, photocopy. Unless otherwise noted, Bible quotations are taken from the Holy Bible, King James Version. Copyright 1982 by Thomas Nelson, Inc., publishers. Used by permission.

Published by:
Cornerstone Publishing
A Division of Cornerstone Creativity Group LLC
Info@thecornerstonepublishers.com
www.thecornerstonepublishers.com
516.547.4999

Author's Contact
For booking to speak at your next event or to order bulk copies of this book please use information below:

Email - thecomos2000@netzero.net
Phone - 832-692-3718

DEDICATION

This book is first of all dedicated to the The father, The Son and the Holy Spirit. Without the inspiration of the Trinity, this book of Love, Mercy and God's Grace could not be possible. We thank you God for all that you have done, are doing and by faith the things we believe you are going to do. Having faith and trust in you Father will get us through anything.

I am also enormously thankful to God for sending me such a loving, caring, respectful and decent wife in Judy Ann Guillory-Como. I didicate this book to her for her untiring efforts of support and co writing of this book of biblical inspirations. I love you very, very much and for your being such a clean and honest person. I thank my God for you and our children and grandchildren everyday.

We also dedicate this book to our children, our first, Courtney Michelle and Brittnay Nicole. We are so proud of the women you have developed into. Dedication to our grandchildren, Jordan Lee, Liam Alexander, Chloe Idara and Kimora Denise. I am further greatful for my two son-n-laws Akan and Michael who are like sons to me. To all of our siblings, their spouses, neices, nephews, uncles, aunts and other relatives, we thank God for you.

To the giants in my life whom inspired me greatly that are now with the Lord. Thank you so much for your guiding hands, Cleveland Sr. and Beatrice my parents, David Sr. and Cecelia my grandparents, Rev. W. W. Como, my uncle for appointing me at the age of 13 to the position of superintendent of sunday school. Rev. Harold L. Guillory, Sr. my father-n-law and my best friend.

I would like to dedicate this book also to my loving husband Dr. Garfield E. Como for all of his love and devotion to me and our family. He has a heart of gold and a love for God and all people. This book is also dedicated to my parents Rev. Harold L. Guillory, Sr. and Virlee Iford Guillory. This dedication goes out to my grandparents Richard and Annie Mae Guillory. I thank God for our union as husband and wife and the family he has given me. Praying that this publication will bless you as much as it was a blessing to produce. May the Lord favor all who read and follow his infallible truths.

Many Blessings,

Dr. Garfield E. & Judy A. Como
Pastor/Founder/Teacher
The Resurrection Church
Richmond, Texas

ACKNOWLEDGMENTS

First I would like to thank Almighty God that sent my savior Jesus Christ that died for my sins and left the Holy Spirit and sits at the right of the Father making intercession for me and all that believe. Without his love, mercy and his grace we could not journey through this barren wilderness. Thank you Father for you anointing power and inspiration.

Secondly, I want to thank my wife Judy for her help with our ministry, along with my daughters Courtney M. Ekpenyong and Brittnay N. Henry for their unending love and support and their work at the church. God has given me a beautiful family and he deserves the praise. I thank him for my son-n-laws Akan I. Ekpenyong and Michael J. Henry and our grandchildren Jordan Lee Bedford, Liam A. Henry, Chloe I. Ekpenyong and Kimora D. Henry. Jordan Lee Bedford my oldest grandson has been my assistant since he was around two years old and he still assist me today at 10 years old. Thank you man. Children are a gift from God.

I would like to acknowledge my Pastors, Dr. Walter K. Berry,Sr., my father in the ministry and wife Vivian Berry of McGee Chapel MBC, Pastor Samuel C. Ammons, my college Pastor of Liberty Baptist Church and the late Dr. L.F. Chaney my grandfather in the ministry of Demascus MBC for their love and support of our ministry. These men had a great deal to do with affording me in ministry with their wisdom and biblical knowledge. Their trust in me has helped to propel me to the place where I am today. Dr. Edward D. Thornton is another man of God and a great teacher of the word of God, that has helped me very significantly.

To the many clergy that have helped me along the way I say thank you and I thank God for you. Dr. Mitchell M. Allen my former sunday school teacher is another christian man and Deacon who helped me along the way and recommended me to become a Deacon.

Finally I give thanks to my friend and publisher of this book at Cornerstone, may the Lord continue to bless your work, family and ministry.

By God's Grace,

Dr. Garfield E. & Judy A. Como,
Pastor/Founder/Teacher
The Resurrection Church
Richmond, Texas

CONTENTS

DEDICATION	5
ACKNOWLEDGMENTS	7
Introduction	13
1. Salvation and Assurance	15
2. Trust and Rescue	17
3. Respect	19
4. Refuge and Strength	21
5. Survival	23
6. Promises and Perseverance	25
7. Salvation and Eternity	28
8. Vengeance and Obedience	30
9. Repentance and Rebound	32
10. Fellowship and Healing	35
11. Protection	38
12. Integrity	41
13. Praise and Worship	43
14. Exaltation and Adoration	45
15. Praise and Thanksgiving	47
16. Protection	49
17. Victory and Strength	52
18. Salvation	54
19. Thanks and Contentment	56
20. Prosperity Joy and Good Health	58

21. Sowing and Reaping	60
22. God's Will	62
23. Volition and Acceptance	64
24. Power of the Holy Spirit	66
25. Exhortation and Help	68
26. Acquitted and Forgiven	70
27. Repentance and Fellowship	72
28. Justice and Forgiveness	75
29. Eternal Security	77
30. Discipline	79
31. Responsibility	81
32. Our Calling	83
33. Salvation	85
34. A Friend and A Father	87
35. Success	89
36. Eternal Value	91
37. Wisdom and Prayer	93
38. Communication	95
39. Steadfastness and Stability	98
40. Deliverance Healing and Restoration	100
41. Guidance	102
42. Obedience and Safety	104
43. Faithfulness	106
44. Transformation	108
45. Protection and Discernment	111
46. Love and Forgiveness	114
47. A Universal Invitation	117
48. Confidence	119

49.	Boldness and Integrity	121
50.	Hope	123
51.	Encouragement	125
52.	Intervention	126
53.	Commission and Instruction	129
54.	Character	131
55.	Patience	134
56.	Love in Action	136
57.	Choices and Persecutions	138
58.	Promises	141
59.	Assurance	143
60.	Choices	145
61.	The Narrow Gate	147
62.	Simple Truth	150
63.	Eternal Rewards	152
64.	Not Guilty	154
65.	Honesty and Justice	156
66.	Searching	158
67.	Waiting and Testing	160
68.	Carrying our Burdens	162
69.	Flesh	164
70.	Patience and Tolerance	166
71.	Worship at Church	168
72.	U-Turns Allowed	170
73.	Straddling the Fence	172
74.	The Light and The way	174
75.	Destiny	176
76.	Heaven's Fix	178

100 BIBLICAL INSPIRATIONS

77.	Giving and Blessings	180
78.	Our Defender and Our Defense	182
79.	The Race and the Reward	184
80.	Agape or Unconditional Love	186
81.	The Character of Love	188
82.	Influences	190
83.	Hypocrisy	192
84.	I Am	194
85.	The Blood	196
86.	Fear and Rest	198
87.	Cares	200
88.	Do not Mix	202
89.	Sovereignty and Providence	204
90.	Happiness	206
91.	The Prize	208
92.	The Challenges	210
93.	Relationship	212
94.	The Will	214
95.	The Word	216
96.	Promise	218
97.	The Great Chasm Closed Forever	220
98.	Salvation	222
99.	Eternity Past	224
100.	The Mind Heart and Soul	226

INTRODUCTION

The word of God needs no introduction but I can invite you to read one of the most compelling books of simple, honest, plain, compelling truths ever written. I say that because many times writers write above the audience instead of at a level that can reach them right where they are and in a simple format.

This book of biblical inspirations will capture your imagination like no other book you have read or will read. It is a must read for all who have struggled, are struggling and will struggle with the issues of life. The book of 2 Timothy 2:15 says " Study to show thyself approved unto God, a workman that needed not be ashamed, rightly dividing the word of truth, ye shall know the truth and the truth shall set you free." Once you start reading this book you will not be able to put it down unless you are an agent of the enemy, Lucifer. It has all of the different topics and solutions of everyday issues we as people go through. Salvation, love, hate, jealousy, marriage, envy, spite, covetousness, malice, forgiveness, unforgiveness, patience, perseverance, joy, peace, assurance, promise and many other issues we face. This book can be read starting from the back, front or middle with ease of understanding. It is relevant for yesterday, today and tomorrow.

It is a very thorough look at what bible doctrine down in the soul can do for those who follow the infallible truths of God. These scriptures and their explanations will come right off the pages at you with conviction and the solutions you need in this world. These biblical inspirations were given to me from the same God that gave inspirations to all of the men that he used as messengers in the bible. I am inspired of men like Abraham, that left his countrymen for a land that God said he would show him, he didn't ask God where? He left in faith. Moses is another that God used for his glory, so he led Israel from their bondage in Egypt to the promised land, being led of God. David a poor shepherd boy, having faith in God, answered his call and slew Goliath with a mere rock and a slingshot. Saul a persecutor of the church, blinded on the road to Damascus and was converted and his name changed to Paul, became a believer in Christ and one of the most prolific writers of the gospel.

In this book you will find lessons on many issues they faced in old testament times, new testament times and in our dispensation of time. This book is inspired by The father, The Son and The Holy Spirit. I think that all who read this book will be blessed by the creator through his word. I give all the Honor, Glory and the Praise to God our Father, Jesus and the Holy Spirit. Amen! May the blessings of the Lord be upon you, your family and your ministry work.

Much Blessings,

Dr. Garfield E. and Judy A. Como,
Pastor/Founder/Teacher
The Resurrection Church, Richmond Texas.

1
SALVATION AND ASSURANCE

But seek ye first the kingdom of God, and his righteousness; and all these things shall be added unto you. **Matthew 6:33**

I sought the Lord and he rescued me from myself. In order for God to help us we have to be on board and in order with his word. How do we get in order or in step with God? He said the first thing we have to do is seek his kingdom which is him that is the righteousness he is speaking of. To be accounted righteous we have to accept the provisions made by God through the Son. We must be born again, that means our thinking must change, we must accept the fact that Jesus is Lord and the only way to the Father.

Above all and anything else, this new birth is a must. Now once this action takes place by us through Christ which is ordained of the Father, all of the things we think we want shall be given us according to our needs being assessed by the Father through the Son. All of our benefits or blessings come from the Father but through the Son, starting with our rebirth. God can only help us when we accept his kingdom connection with Christ. Man must understand that according to God's plan for man , it all starts and ends with the Son by the will of the Father.

In order to be blessed and to receive the blessings of God, we have to follow his plan. When we deviate from the plan that's where we fall out of fellowship and miss our scheduled blessings during this period of lost fellowship with Christ. Our natural minds and affections we have for temporal things cause this lost of fellowship. Now don't misunderstand, God knows we are flesh and as apostle Paul said, "there is no good thing that dwells in my flesh." Still God is there to help us when we fall, that was the main purpose of Jesus coming to save man from himself.

Now just because we have accepted the blood doesn't mean that we have an open door to do as we please without consequences. But, God is faithful, hang on to the promise and not the world. The world will tangle you up and keep you confused, but the spirit will loose you and set you free. Amen Saints!

2
TRUST AND RESCUE

Behold, the eye of the Lord is upon them that fear him, upon them that hope in his mercy.

Psalms 33:18

The Lord helps all those that respect him and depend upon his mercy. The fear of the Lord is the beginning of Wisdom. This means that when we reverence the Lord, we accept his Sovereignty and Divine authority. We realize from our spiritual knowledge that he is the power that created all and controls all. The Lord is not a dictator but a loving and merciful God.

This proof is in the fact that he gave everyone of us volition or the freedom to choose.

He said in his word " Come to me all who are heavy laden and burden down and I will give you rest. He knew that it would be impossible for us to lose ourselves from the shackles and entanglements of life, so he made a way for us through our trust in him. When we face the fact of reality that he made us and not we ourselves, we can realize by faith that he wills good for us through his Son.

The plan of God included man before he created us and this world. His love is far more intense and reaching than our intellect can comprehend. God further intends for man to prosper in this life but this can only happen if we follow him and apply his word in our lives. The scripture declares that " The eyes of the Lord are upon the righteous and his ears are open to their cry." This means that he is watching over his children and he is waiting on us to ask him for his help.

When we depend and trust in him for everything it keeps us away from the many dangers and issues of life. That scripture in Psalm 34 that says" Let the words of my mouth and the meditation of my heart be acceptable to you, my redeemer and my strength." This is a simple request by the petitioner that what he had in his heart and mind would be accepted by God. Everything that comes out of our mouths are not praiseworthy or acceptable. Following Christ keeps us in fellowship with him and keeps us out of harm's way. Amen Saints! Have a blessed day.

3
RESPECT

Let no corrupt communication proceed out of your mouth, but that which is good to the use of edifying, that it may minister grace unto the hearers.**Ephesians 4:29**

How to communicate without corruption from the tongue. Soft words turn away wrath. If two people are speaking to each other with foul and abusive communication, then there is no understanding that prevails. When we communicate with the intent to encourage, forgive , ask for forgiveness with patience and long suffering, only then do we edify one another and bring glory to the Father.

Two people can't talk at the same time if the intent is to bring understanding and peace. soft words means that our intent is to bring calm to a disruptive situation that has gotten out of hand. When the waters on the sea of Tiberius had gotten out of hand and Jesus had been awaken, he didn't scream at the disciples or the turbulent waves. He simply said "peace be still" it calmed the disciples nerves and the water became normal again.

If you are having a tough time with someone or you are in an untenable situation, try the methods of Christ. The remedies of Christ are far better and longer lasting than those of the world. Remember who is the prince of the world for yet a little while, then Christ will come back and show who is and has always been in charge. The enemies job is to kill, steal and destroy. We support the enemies cause when we can't communicate properly with one another as believers.

The unbeliever seems to be fairing better than the believer only because in many cases we fail to apply what we have been taught from the scriptures. What good is knowledge if we don't ever apply what we know. Knowledge is power, but the knowledge we receive from the world is short circuited because of our conforming to this world. The knowledge we receive from God through Christ that gave us the Holy Spirit is sound, sure, profitable, expedient and everlasting.

Anybody can be loud, crude, rude, obnoxious, disrespectful and mean spirited but it takes work to try and bring peace and resolution to uncomfortable situations and disagreeable people. Jesus said " As much as possible, try to live peacefully among men (people). He knew that it might be impossible in some situations and with some people, even our own family, but he says we should give it our best Christian effort. Life is hard but the yoke of God is easy and his burdens are light. He is the way in every situation we find ourselves in and the solution that fixes them, when we follow his guide through the Holy Spirit. Amen Saints! Have a blessed day.

4
REFUGE AND STRENGTH

There is none holy as the Lord: for there is none beside thee: neither is there any rock like our God. **1 Samuel 2:2**

Who but the Lord created all that we see, even the things we can't see? He is a rock in a weary land. We can count on the strength of God during periods of weakness or distress. There is no God like our God. None can rescue or respond like him. When mine enemies and my foes came to eat up (destroy me) my flesh, they stumbled and they fell (were destroyed) who destroys your enemies but the hand of God?

No one has a more sturdy hand than God. No one can rescue, forgive, save, deliver, heal or bring you through like him. There is healing, power and deliverance in that name. He is the only one true and living God our Father. I will lift mine eyes unto the hills from whence cometh my help(the solution to my problems). When we hold on to our stronghold, which is in Christ, the storms of life shouldn't shake us.

Now the concerns we have are normal but our help is uncommon and comes from a Holy God that reigns from above. He sends the seasons in part to remind us of his power and authority and his providence over everything and everyone. The Lord is not like man who abuses his power but rather uses his power for his glory and our good. There is no God like him and none more Holy than him. His judgements are good and righteous.

We can depend on him and he won't fail us. Man sometimes will promise one thing with no intent on fulfilling his promise, but God does exactly what he says he will or won't do. Whatever you may be going through, have faith that he will hear you and bring it to pass. While he is working things out be content. Paul said" I've learned to be content (understand, accept) in whatever condition I found myself in." Learning comes from experience and experience comes from going through something.

The most meaningful experiences we can have comes from and through the things that the Father has willed for us to go through, with emphasis on the word "through". Whatever you need, depend on the Rock of our Salvation. Amen Saints! . Have a blessed day.

5
SURVIVAL

For I the Lord thy God will hold thy right hand, saying unto thee, Fear not; I will help thee.

Isaiah 41:13

He comforts me and holds my hand and directs me through the storms of life. Life is filled with twists and turns, surprises and new beginnings. When God holds our right hand it shows our standing with God. It's funny, when we are walking with our children we tell them, hold my right hand. It's something about the strength and power of the right.

When we examine things or people, we make sure as best we can to make sure that the right motives are involved. Jesus sits at the right of his Father making intercessions for us. You've heard the term, you better straighten up and fly right. In other words, you were being admonished to stop doing wrong and to turn and do what is right in the sight of the one issuing the statement. When God speaks to us, he lets us know that he is the one that brings us through whatever life throws our way.

Many times in the Old Testament when he spoke to his prophets like Isaiah and others, and they heard his voice or that of the angels. He said do not be afraid, because he knew that the sound of his voice brought about fright before the calming of his voice. He speaks to us today with that same voice, but it is done in us through the Holy Spirit. It can sometimes be alarming, depending on what it is guiding us to do and yet calming when we recognize its power to heal and deliver.

Only God can bring us safely through the storms and issues of life. He can't help us if we won't let him hold our hand. He can't possibly hold the hands of them whom he doesn't know. How can he come to know us? Only through our acceptance of his offer of the Holy Spirit through his Son. Accept his Son and allow him to hold your hand through the journey of life and let him lead you all the way to heaven in that day.

6
PROMISES AND PERSEVERANCE

Behold, I will send my messenger, and he shall prepare the way before me: and the Lord, whom ye seek, shall suddenly come to his temple, even the messenger of the covenant, whom ye delight in: behold, he shall come, saith the Lord of hosts. **Malachi 3:1**

I will confirm for you in person what you were told by my messengers! The purpose of God's messengers were to announce his coming and to give man a chance to turn right and go straight. Man's problems have always been a combination of what he thought in his mind and what he allowed himself to do in his flesh.

For many throughout the Bible, disobedience has been our downfall. Even us today, disobedience and arrogance is what has man in this fault line with the Father. We have been told like Israel that the Savior would come to save man from himself because of his sin nature. The forewarnings have been used as an alert for us to get right, but our fascination with this world and its folly has caused man to walk foul in the sight of God.

Israel walked foul in the sight of God and had to be shown who was in charge, now, America who does as Israel did before God is now being brought to task because of their disobedience. Now this Christ that the messengers spoke about that would come and teach in the temple, he came and will come again, and he is on his way back.

The New Covenant that he brought to this world then, still stands today as our guide through the Holy Spirit, for us to live by today and until he comes again. People change but the word of God doesn't. The hard roads or the challenges we face only leads us to a better place, when we place our trust and confidence in the one who came and is on the way back. That old 100 song says " I will trust in the Lord until I die." This means that no matter what I may have to go through, my faith tells me that eventually in this world I will be alright and I will be even better on the other side.

God promised his children that we would experience the fat of the land in the land of the living. Though the ride here may be rough sometimes but God's plan is to take you above the turbulence and allow you to experience some of the comforts he has planned for you. Much of your teaching is being overlooked by you, because you disregard what the Holy Spirit is trying to tell you.

Be still, listen to the Holy Spirit and follow its guidance. The Holy Spirit is in reality, God speaking and leading us if we will listen. God decided to come and live in us through the Holy Spirit. Just as a father guides his children so does our Heavenly Father guide us through the Holy Ghost. Are you listening? Amen Saints! Have a blessed day.

7
SALVATION AND ETERNITY

For by grace are ye saved through faith; and that not of yourselves: it is the gift of God:
Ephesians 2:8

I know it was the Lord that saved me! The unmerited favor of God is what saved us. We could not work, offer or do anything that would merit this free gift from God. His love overruled what he saw in sinful man and willed in the heart of God to save man through his Son, Jesus Christ.

This season that we celebrate the birth of Christ is all about the redemptive work on the cross by the Messiah through the will of the Father. When something is given to us that we can't work for, it falls into the gift category. The plan of God for man was to have him submit of his own free will into accepting this gift of Christ as his Savior and Lord.

In the fellowship of Christ we began to understand that we are created beings dependent on Christ but with a free will to choose as we please. In God's plan he doesn't leave to chance our not knowing the penalty we receive for making the wrong choices. God has sent angels, prophets, teachers, preachers and Son to show us what the results would be from our choices.

The volitional choice of faith saves us by his grace, which is the will of the Father. The Lord says " I would that none should perish, but all come into repentance. This means that the will of the Father is for none of us to die without him and go to an eternal destination in hell but to accept the redemptive work of his Son so that we would have eternal life through Christ and live eternally with God in the New Jerusalem. But all of this depends on the choice we make.

The Lord says, "Choose you this day whom you will serve. "Me or the devil? The choice is really ours, so choose rightly and don't complain if you make the wrong choice. It's totally up to us, where we will end up at the close of this life. Amen Saints! Choose God's gift of Christ through faith and live eternally with God.

8
VENGEANCE AND OBEDIENCE

The Lord shall fight for you, and ye shall hold your peace. **Exodus 14:14**

The Lord is mighty in battle and is the victor in every fight. Who can stand against the Lord? Stand and watch the salvation(strength, hand and strong arm) of the Lord. He is the one that makes our enemies our footstools. Vengeance is mine says the Lord, I will repay(overtake or settle the score).

All through the Bible from beginning to the end, when it came to victory over our enemies, it was God's hand that brought his children through. Israel was a prime example of how God fought their battles. From Egypt to the land of Canaan or the promised land, it was God whose mighty hand overcame their troubles, whether it was lack of water, food or a physical enemy.

Along the journey on their way to the promised land, they met numerous oppositions and challenges like the

Amalekites, Moabites, Amorites and many others. Their protector and battle axe was above them in a cloud by day and a pillar of fire by night, leading, providing and protecting the nation of Israel. They were God's chosen nation. The same God that chose them has also chosen you. The question is. Have you accepted his offer of Salvation and provision and protection through his Son? If you have, you have the same promises as Israel.

The access to the provisions and promises are through his Son. When the Lord is busy fighting our battles, he instructs us to hold our peace(tongue and be careful of what we say). This battle is not ours but the Lords. The scripture tells us that we are not to overcome evil with evil but to overcome evil with good.

The take away from this lesson is to let someone who is a precision fighter handle your struggles or battles for you. He is not a man but God. So let go and let God do it today. He gets glory when we stand on faith knowing that he is there and wants to help us win. Be strong in the Lord and the power of his might. Amen Saints! Have a victorious day and journey with and through Christ.

9
REPENTANCE AND REBOUND

Create in me a clean heart, O God; and renew a right spirit within me. **Psalms 51:10**

When we fall and repent, he cleans us up for his continued kingdom use. When a baby soils its diaper, you don't throw the baby away with the diaper, you clean him up and continue to love and train him. God knows that because we are flesh, we are going to make some mistakes. That's why he gave Moses the law for Israel to follow including Moses. But that was what the problem was, the law was weak so he sent Jesus and the New Covenant so that man's sin could be overcome through the shed blood of his Son Jesus Christ.

God has always given man a way out through his spoken word, but it's a choice that we have to personally make if we want this family relationship and peace with God. People make choices everyday about many different things, many times without really thinking about the consequences.

We have to continually watch our motives and our way of thinking on the issues we face in this life.

Our journey can get complexed, distracting, confusing, overwhelming, discouraging and filled with despair, but the answer is simple. Jesus! He is the way, the truth and the life. He is our way from the snare of the fowler. The palmist ask God to create in him a clean heart and to renew a right spirit within him. Cleansing comes from admission and repentance. You can't be cleaned spiritually until you repent, that a must do action by you. Then to be renewed in the spirit you must have the spirit of Christ in you.

The problem with many believers is that they have done some things right like asked Jesus to come into their lives. They have Salvation, but they have fallen out of fellowship with Christ because of sin and have not repented. The only way for this psalm to be answered for you or anyone, is that you have to know Christ, not know of him, but know him through the blood by receiving him as your personal Lord and Savior. I know it was the blood that saved me. Now you have to apply the scripture 1 John 1:9. This where the cleansing power and renewal of the spirit comes into play for the believer.

The heart is desperately wicked or evil and it devises many wrong doings but the assurance of its cleansing and renewal results from the acknowledgment of our sin and repentance. If you want God to fix your problems you have to face them and not hide or blame them on somebody else. Remember Adam blamed the women Eve that God gave him, but Adam actually took a bite of the forbidden fruit! You ate the fruit so go on and admit it and ask God to clean you up and correct the way you think and do things.

He is waiting to answer you, make the call. There is no human creature that God created that is qualified to escape making that call. The scripture says " For all (everybody) have sinned and fallen short of the glory of God." Romans 3:23. The world needs to pray this prayer, because it certainly has fallen away from our creator. The scripture declares that " though you are in the world, be not a part of it." Don't conform to this world but be he transformed (let God change your mindset, your attitude and polluted thinking) Amen Saints! Have a blessed day all day.

10
FELLOWSHIP AND HEALING

If my people, which are called by my name, shall humble themselves, and pray, and seek my face, and turn from their wicked ways; then will I hear from heaven, and will forgive their sin, and will heal their land. **2 Chronicles 7:14**

When we become humble, repent and pray, that's when God answers us. The people that God is speaking about is not only Israel, even though at the time that's who he was talking about. This promise is good for us today and all those coming behind us until Christ comes back. The problem is that the Christian believers of that time and even us today are guilty of continuing in trespasses and sins against the Father.

How many times have you been told when you were growing up to stop doing what you were doing, that was wrong in the sight of your parents? They told you that if you didn't get it together you would eventually suffer the consequences of your actions. God said to Israel through

Moses and the Mosaic Law, that his people Israel needed to take heed to the law handed down to Moses on Mount Sinai.

The coming of Jesus and the new covenant that he brought was and is the guide for us to follow and not break. Just as God said in this scripture " if my people." Who are God's people? Those who have accepted and will accept the blood of Christ. What is God asking us as his people to do, as he also asked his chosen nation of Israel? He is simply saying, first you must become humble. Realize and acknowledge that you have done wrong and to whom you have done wrong. Then after you have humbled yourself and are sorrowful for what you have done, now pray and turn from your wicked ways and seek his face, ask for his forgiveness.

The scripture says " Humble yourselves before the mighty hand of God." This means be still, lose your arrogance and realize you are standing under the authority of God. Israel's false sense of security like ours, was they believed that since they were God's chosen people, they had privileges, and part of that is somewhat true. But the truth of this matter was that in spite of their being, like us, his children, God expects us to govern ourselves according to the standard he set for Israel under the Mosaic Law and to us in this present day and going forward until he comes, to live under the New Covenant that Christ ushered in.

In humbling ourselves and praying, we must turn back to him. Which mean we can no longer walk our own way and do our own thing. We must follow the plan that God has laid out for his children through the Law then and through Christ and the New Covenant now and going forward until the coming of Christ to rapture the church out of this world. The Bible says " Blessed (happy) is he who is a part (saved) of the second coming." When we follow this mandate to the letter, the scripture says " then I will answer them(solve their problems)."

The trouble with this world and God's children is, because he has prospered us so, many have turned their backs on God and are walking their own way. Prosperity can sometimes cripple us to the point where we feel we don't need God until we need God, and that is what causes our problems. America has been walking in its own way for too long and now what you see is God exposing America for its walking or falling away from God.

Now if we and America and this world, turn back to God in humble submission and honestly pray and repent. The Lord says he will answer us and solve our issues, just as he did Israel. The sad commentary is that everyone that left Egypt, didn't make it to the promised land (Canaan). The good news for us in our dispensation of the time in which we live is, that once we receive salvation, we will make it to the New Jerusalem. But when we get out of step, the Lord will pull the covers off of us and spank us right here in the land of the living.

Don't let anyone tell you that you can lose your salvation! If they try, refer them to John 3:16 which says" For God so loved the world that he gave his only begotten Son, that whosoever believeth in him, should not perish, but have everlasting life." There are other supportive scriptures, but this one is most recognized and quoted. Turn from what you may be doing and allow God to help you through your troubles. He is waiting for your turnaround. Amen Saints! Have a blessed evening.

11
PROTECTION

What shall we then say to these things? If God be for us, who can be against us? **Romans 8:31**

There is nothing stronger or powerful enough to overcome the love, mercies and grace of God! When I think about where he has brought me from, I can't help but stand in awe and say thank you. Thank you because, if it had not been for his love, mercy and his grace, where would I or any of his children be? Thank you God for picking me up out of the dung hills of this world and placing me solidly back on my feet.

My flesh had caused me to slip because I lost my focus on you. Sometimes in life when we get a little ahead with some of the trappings of life, money, houses, land, cars, businesses and what we think are the markings of success, we lose focus. It's easy to slip when you think you have it all and you have no need of any assistance from anybody. We can let our conscious or subconscious mind fool us into thinking we have made it.

Maybe you have somewhat made it from a worldly viewpoint. But you haven't, that's the enemies way of causing a chasm between you and God and it can cause you to become prideful and cause you to fall and lose your way. Now, don't get me wrong, there is nothing wrong in accumulating some of the things in life you want. The danger is when we lose focus on the provider of those gifts. The scripture says " every good and precious gift comes from above." If God didn't want us to have them, believe me when I tell you, you wouldn't have them.

Sometimes for some people, when they get too much to fast, they believe it's them and not the blessings of God and they lose themselves in and to themselves, and that Saints is the nemesis of man. Self pride and arrogance. Pride cometh before the fall. It's alright to have great personal esteem for oneself, but not to the point of pious, especially arrogance. The scripture declares " man ought not to think more highly of himself than he ought to (the place where God feels you understand where it all comes from) him." God does not want you to walk around with your head hung down all of the time with low self esteem(letting the enemy make you think you're nobody) when you are in fact, more than a conqueror in Christ!

The scripture declares that " I can do all things (make it through day by day) through Christ that strengthens me." Now that's some good news for living a balanced life and not allowing ourselves to fall by way of the devil in our arrogance. The formula for long lasting success starts and ends with Christ which is the word. When the world shows us the bright lights it can be very unsettling to someone who has lived a quiet life, now it appears you can have all that you never had and always thought you wanted. The world's lights can be your downfall but the light of Christ can save us.

When we choose Christ, the world somehow seems to turn on us, but that's alright too. Our refuge and our strength is found in the promise of God that declares " If God is for us(he holds us, keeps us and supplies all that we need or could imagine) who can stand against us (or defeat us)? Nobody!!!!! Amen Saints! Only God can stick to a promise like this. Hold on to his unchanging hand in this changing world! Enjoy your life that he has ordained for you and you only! Have a blessed day and enjoy your worship Sunday.

12
INTEGRITY

For whatsoever things were written aforetime were written for our learning, that we through patience and comfort of the scriptures might have hope.

Now the God of patience and consolation grant you to be like minded one toward another according to Christ Jesus: **Romans 15:4-5**

When we fashion ourselves after Christ, we become like minded to him. Christian integrity is a characteristic of Christ. It allows us to see things through the eyes of Christ in the indwelling of The Holy Spirit. Without the Holy Spirit we cannot see our way past impatience, indulgences, selfishness, self pride, unforgiveness and all of the things that war against the Holy Spirit.

The Spirit is the thing that calms us down and allows us to recognize the things that causes despair and irritations in our lives. Prayer changes the landscapes of life. There are different playing fields that pop up in our lives as we travel through this barren wilderness we call life's journey. The patience it takes to get through the many issues in life we will face can only be achieved through the Spirit and not from the flesh.

The flesh is enmity with God. The flesh is contrary to the will of God. The Spirit sent from God through the Son is the key that allows the joys of the Father to permeate our lives and our very souls. Oh the joy and happiness that we find when we yield over complete control and guidance to the Spirit sent from above.

Peace is very hard to find and maintain in the world we live in, but it is achievable only through Christ our Lord. The formula to take hold of this peace is through fervent prayer and request to the Father. Our thoughts should reflect on the things above, even though we are in the world. When we conform to the world, we get the things of the world that are sometimes good and ultimately not the things we need.

The test is when we allow for our transformation by the changing of the mind or the way we think, we realize the importance of the prize we are fighting for. What is that prize? The high calling of Christ Jesus. Our eternal destiny in heaven with God. We should always pray and not faint, when we think that our prayers are going unanswered, that's the window the enemy gets in on us and starts his devilish acts of torments. Keep knocking on the door and eventually it will be opened unto you, if you don't quit and give up and give in. Amen Saints! Great word for a troubled world and a troubled people.

13
PRAISE AND WORSHIP

I will praise thee, O Lord, with my whole heart;
I will shew forth all thy marvellous works.

Psalms 9:1

I will praise you and tell of your goodness, mercies and your grace. Everything good in our lives God did it. It was not because of me but because of his unfailing love, mercies and his grace. When I think about what God has done, what he is doing and by faith what he will do, I can't do anything other than stand in awe and praise and thank him for his marvelous works and his grace.

As the dawning of each new day begins and we find ourselves in the middle of new and fresh blessings from above, that should indicate to us that God has smiled on us and set us free to do new kingdom works for his glory and our good. The enemy is going to throw rocks or troubles sometimes during this reading or after, but remember, God is our rock and he will handle the enemy. Just continue to walk in the gentle flow of the living waters of God and bless and help someone today regardless of their rough exterior or hard hearts.

God can change a stony heart, our job is to plant the seeds of forgiveness and compassion and God will honor our requests and water them so that they may ultimately grow for his kingdom use. We are just seed planters and not the creators of growth. In our own lives, we can only sow our seeds and God waters us with his living waters and causes us to grow for his glory and use which creates good in us.

I pray that someone will receive this this morning and pass this along. Look at our world and see how it is toiling and going in the wrong direction. The only thing that can turn things around for us just like it was for the nation of Israel, God's chosen people is God.

The world needs to make a u-turn and go back to God and let him lead the way. He is the way and the only way back to safe and Holy ground. He told Moses " Moses, take your sandals off you are standing on Holy ground." We need to do the same. Our Holy ground that we stand on or should be standing on is the word of God. Amen Saints! Repost and share if you can. Have a wonderfully blessed day and have a Happy Thanksgiving. Remember that someone is without, share what God has blessed you with and be blessed.

14
EXALTATION AND ADORATION

O Lord, thou art my God; I will exalt thee, I will praise thy name; for thou hast done wonderful things; thy counsels of old are faithfulness and truth. **Isaiah 25:1**

My trust is in the faithfulness and promises of God. When God says it's so, you can count on it. When he says it's done, it done. When the model prayer says" thy will be done" it simply means that, what he wills for heaven and earth cannot be stopped. The devil in hell has no authority over God.

What the Father promises has already been done, all we have to do is learn how to access the benefits. Many people waste so much time trying to figure out with their natural minds what has already been laid out in scripture for our benefit. When the flesh tries to come against the spirit, that's where the trouble begins for man with God. Our flesh is enmity against God and it cannot win.

God's plan is for the soul to survive and live through the

guidance of the Holy Spirit. The first step to overcoming the will of the flesh is to declare God to be your God and you accomplish this through belief in his Son Jesus Christ our Lord. Priceless are the promises, strength and application of his word. When we stand on the word we have the full backing of the Father in Heaven. Nothing can befall us unless God decides to send us through a battery of test.

The only way you can come through some medical crisis is by of a battery of test. Now don't get medical test and spiritual test mixed up. Both successes come from the hand of God. If it is left up to the enemy, he would keep you sick and feeble minded, downtrodden, hopeless and in despair. The scripture declares " while I was yet speaking the Lord heard me and answered my prayers." So we can conclude that prayer changes things and are there for our benefit of communication with the Father.

If Jesus the perfect sacrifice had not come in obedience to the Father and hung, bled, and died and rose, we would not have the privilege to go straight to the Father with our request or problems or concerns. So declare it today that Jesus is your personal Lord and Savior and his Father is your God and thank him for the Holy Spirit through his Son. Now you can rest assured that he can handle whatever the enemy throws our way. Amen Saints! Somebody needs to hear this and know that Jesus is the only way to Salvation!!! Have a blessed evening and have a happy thanksgiving everybody.

15
PRAISE AND THANKSGIVING

Thus will I bless thee while I live: I will lift up my hands in thy name. **Psalms 63:4**

How blessed we are to have a God that provides like you! It is by his love and provision that we are able to say thank you and lift our hands and sing praises to his Holy name. It is not us but the love of the Father through the Son that we are alive and have a home here and our heavenly home in the New Jerusalem.

We should be thankful certainly in this season of thanksgiving that he has sustained us through all the travail going on in our world today. There should be singing and dancing and praise for all that he has already done as we get ready by faith to receive what he is going to do.

We should thank God for the Lamb and the blood without which there would be no remission of sins and peace with God. I am thankful today because of the blood and my relationship with the Father, Son and Holy Ghost. My hope is built on the sustaining promises of God through the Son.

I am thankful that we have a Heavenly Father whose love is unconditional and he accepts all who have accepted Son. Choose Christ today and be thankful for his provisions and the life that we share in Christ Jesus our Lord and Savior. I am thankful for my family and for you the body of Christ. Amen Saints! Have a wonderfully blessed Thanksgiving with Christ and your families.

16
PROTECTION

But thou, O Lord, art a shield for me; my glory, and the lifter up of mine head. **Psalms 3:3**

The Lord is our help, protection and our Savior. For all those who have chosen Christ, he has become your protector and your ark of safety and our hope in this chaotic world we live in. It was God's choice through our parents to bring us here for his glory and it is also his choice to be our shield or protection from the enemy.

The Lord's hand of coverage is not upon us if we have not taken the step in choosing his Son as our Lord. When we choose the Lord, we have chosen God and the Holy Ghost also which represents the Holy Trinity, God the Father, God the Son and God the Holy Ghost. It is the Lord that lifts our countenance when we are buffeted by the ills and pressures of this life. He is the lifter of them who are heavy laden and burdened down.

Our spirits are set free only because of a forgiving and

compassionate God. The world has no compassion for us, but God through the Holy Spirit given to us through the Son is our hiding place of refuge while he restores our strength and the direction when the enemy knocks us off our path. In times of trouble and indecision, we must flee or run to the rock of our salvation, the flowing fountain and the restoration of our souls.

The living water is the only thing that can restore, refresh and deliver us in our relationship with Christ. The enemy wants you to believe that the temporary travail we experience will last always and it won't! Why? Because God does not intend for us to last any longer in the storm than is necessary for us to learn from it. The duration is left up to us.

The duration has already been ordered, just as it was for Israel in their exile under the Babylonians. I am so glad that trouble don't last always. In spite of Israel's missteps, the Lord honors his Covenant. In spite of our missteps and bad decisions, he honors his covenants with us. Many of our troubles are not from God or the devil, but are self induced misery we bring on ourselves from our own misbehavior because of our not applying the Bible doctrine we have learned but forget to pull it out from our store house because we are not quite ready to stop sinning!

Why would we do that? Because the devil keep making you feel that you can stop when you want! Ask the liar, the drug addict, the whoremonger, the cheater to name a few. The all thought like many of you, I can stop when I want to. Only to find out that they couldn't, only God our shield and buckler, our protector could bring us out and through because the devil would still have you caught up in you mess. His grace is sufficient and his mercies are endless and his love is unconditional. That is our key to success and survival in this life. Turn your life over to our unchanging God in this constantly changing world. Amen Saints! God bless you and keep you is our prayer.

17
VICTORY AND STRENGTH

But thanks be to God, which giveth us the victory through our Lord Jesus Christ.
1 Corinthians. 15:57

There is victory in Jesus Christ our Lord. We are more than conquerors through Christ. The enemies plan is for us to fall for his temporary trappings he places before us. Misplaced successes, false sense of those people who appear to be our friends and on our side, only they fail us when the chips are down and you don't provide them what they want from you. The Father operates for us from the vantage point of provision and need and not our want and our greed.

The world deals to us many times over, failures, heartache and pain, because we look to the wrong thing or people to solve our problems. Christ says " Come to me (not the world) all who are heavy laden and burden down (going through life's issues) and I will give you rest (safety, assurances, success and a way out)." This promise from

Christ points us as to how to overcome the difficulties and struggles of this life. He says be not overcome with evil but overcome evil with good.

The race is not give to the swift (cunning) or fleet of foot but to him that endureth (perseveres or last) to the end. The person that can hold on until either Christ comes back and receives us or we die in Christ and rise at his second coming to get the redeemed. Everlasting victory we receive in this life even the victory over sin and death comes from and through Christ Jesus.

The enemy wants you to think your victories come from your doing, that's a lie from the pits of hell. 1 Corinthians 15:57 says our victory comes from and through Christ Jesus our Lord. Now if he is not your Lord, then your victories or temporary victories and are supplied by the enemy that wants to bring you to hell and he will if you accept his lies. Accept Christ today if you haven't already and experience true and lasting, fulfilling victories in this life and the life eternal to come in the New Jerusalem. Amen Saints! Have a blessed day all day.

18
SALVATION

For the grace of God that bringeth salvation hath appeared to all men. **Titus 2:11**

By his grace we are saved through faith. We are undeserving of his grace but because of his unconditional love he has sent the Son to save all that accept him. Jesus said" I would that none should perish (die and go to hell) but all would come to repentance." God will is for his creation to be saved but his creation has to personally welcome his salvation through faith and ask of him to be their Lord and Savior.

It's just that simple but many will not do this simple act of faith. In reality we control our fate in this regard to salvation. It's a personal choice that every individual has the volitional choice to make. The scripture says " As many as received him they gained the right to become sons and daughters of the most high." What does that mean? It means that everyone and anyone that accepts Christ would be saved and set apart for the Masters use.

There is no risk in accepting the offer of Salvation other than the loss of eternity with Christ because of our failure to accept his offer of Salvation. We can't merit his grace but we can receive the rewards of his grace. What are the benefits? Salvation, The Holy Spirit and the New Jerusalem and God's hand of favor on your life in the land of the living. Amen Saints!

19
THANKS AND CONTENTMENT

Now therefore, our God, we thank thee, and praise thy glorious name. **1 Chronicles 29:13**

We give thanks to God always for his marvelous works. In all things we should give God praise. The Apostle Paul said " I've learned to be content in whatever condition (circumstance) I found myself in. In our daily lives we find ourselves inundated with many situations and circumstances. The test is how do you handle yourself in the midst of your trials. Praise is one sure way to take your mind off carnal things or worldly problems and focus on things above through praise. Christ said " In everything you thank me." All things work to the good of them who love God are called according to his purpose.

Our praise goes up and the benefit is the blessings that are sent down to us from the hand of God. Praise is something that is constant. Praise can be hard or challenging for us when are in the middle of travail, despair, hardships, failures, loss, divorce, separation and many issues of life. In spite of these probabilities, we should still have the strength and faith to go on and the will to continue to praise him for what he has already done and by faith know that he will bring us through again.

Many blessings I have experienced have come right after challenges and much travail. When we focus on the problem we can't see the need to praise because our problems keeps us out of the right focus. God is bigger than any problem you have or could have in the future. Stand on the promises and continue in praise and receive the provision. Amen Saints! Have a blessed night.

20
PROSPERITY JOY AND GOOD HEALTH

Beloved, I wish above all things that thou mayest prosper and be in health, even as thy soul prospereth. **3 John 1:2**

The will of God is for his creation to prosper and to have good health and to do good. It doesn't make very much sense for the flesh to do good and the soul doesn't. The flesh is temporary but the soul is eternal. The question is. Where do you want your soul to rest and how can it help you in this life.

The soul is the residence of the Holy Spirit and that is what Christ is coming back to get, not the flesh. So why mind the things of the flesh and ignore the Spirit? Why put so much attention to something that fades and less to that which will live forever. When we mind the things of the flesh we subconsciously disobey the guidance of the spirit which cause enmity between us and God.

The main reason we were created is to glorify and obey God and he supplies all that we need to more than survive this chaotic and dismal world. The Lord says " though you are in the world, be not a part of it. No matter how good it looks, don't conform to the standards of this world. Narrow is the gate that leads to life and few find it but broad is the way that leads to doom and destruction.

God is not requiring us to live our lives in a humdrum fashion of despair and depression. He wants us to live as to Christ and he will give us all the joy and happiness we can handle here in the land of the living. You have heard that Blondes have more fun but I tell you that all you need is faith and daily application of the word and by his grace there is no greater fulfillment than his blessings. Everyone wants to prosper but the key to prosperity and health is in our fellowship with Christ. Christ runs and has authority over the blessings room. Every good and every precious gift comes from above. All provisions are ordered from above and delivered through his promises by faith. Amen

21
SOWING AND REAPING

Be not deceived; God is not mocked: for whatsoever a man soweth, that shall he also reap. **Galatians 6:7**

We get out of this life what we put in. A farmer doesn't plant corn and expect cabbage to be his harvest from the corn he planted. Just as the person who ask Christ to be his Lord and Savior, expects eternal life or Salvation through Christ. He doesn't expect hell as his harvest from his profession of faith. We have to be deliberate and exact with what we sow or plant. Our harvest or gain is tied directly to what we plant. Galatians 6:7.

Many will try and convince you that our harvest is immediately after our planting. There is an incubation period or a waiting period before our harvest. After we sow, we have to nurture what has been sown. We have to cultivate and make sure we give our planting a chance to harvest. Many want or expect instant results, but it doesn't work like that. We made or make God wait on us for our turnaround but we want him to be instantly responsive when we make our request and then question him when we think it takes too long to get our expected results from Heaven.

Now the question is, just what are you planting and just what are you expecting from your works? If we sow or plant good seeds of hope then we can expect and we will gain or harvest good from the works of our hands from the promises of God. Galatians 6:7. When we sow evil seeds we can expect to receive nothing other than a bad harvest.

Nothing good can come from evil. Evils nature is not a yielder of anything good. Conversely, good cannot yield anything evil because evil is not in the nature of good. Good yields good and evil yields evil! Now the enemy can use evil against you and the Father can turn it around for your good. The supervisor on your job can do you wrong and it is apparent to everybody, then God steps in and the supervisor is released from his position of authority and you get the position.

We never know where and how our harvest or blessings are going to flow from or through but the Father knows. Just remain humble and pray and keep the faith and God will bring it to pass. Plant good seeds and keep pleasant thoughts and maintain a Christian attitude and watch your manifest through God's will. Amen Saints! This is how you get good harvest.

22
GOD'S WILL

For the earth shall be filled with the knowledge of the glory of the Lord, as the waters cover the sea.**Habakkuk 2:14**

The hand of God covers everything and has authority over it all even the covering of the seas and everything in it. Everywhere you look and all that you see, even the unseen is filled or originated by him. His presence is everywhere all at the same time, which represents his omnipresence, he knows about everything, which is his omnipotence, he is all knowing, which represents that he is omniscient.

There is no thought you can have, no place you can go, no one you can be with, no scheme you can come up with or anything that he is not aware of. He is the only true and living God our Father. He wants to have a personal relationship with you and be the guiding force and at the control center of your life.

He wills for you to have a good life here in the land of the living and his ultimate destiny for your life is to live eternally with him in the life to come in his heavenly kingdom in the New Jerusalem. He is the only one that has your best interest at heart and wants to fill you up with his Spirit. Our lives are in his hands and he wills for us to experience the fat(good, prosperity) of the land in the land of the living, while you are alive in the flesh but controlled by the Spirit! Amen Saints!

23
VOLITION AND ACCEPTANCE

For all flesh is as grass, and all the glory of man as the flower of grass. The grass withereth, and the flower thereof falleth away:

1 Peter 1:24

The flesh is temporary, just as the beauty of the green grass and the fragrant flowers. We are here today and gone tomorrow but the soul which houses the Spirit is our gateway to live with Christ forever, those whom he knows. How do we know him except for our asking him to come and live in us through the Holy Spirit given to us the day we accepted him as our personal Lord and Savior.

When Christ came to this earth, he brought with him a New Covenant. This New Covenant has at its very core the volitional mandate of a personal relationship. When we accept Christ, we are no longer that old person, but a new creature, bound for a new horizon in the new Jerusalem. No longer tormented by the ills of this world, but protected by an eternal God because of the shed blood of The Son of God, Christ the Lord!!!

We should understand that beauty fades but the word of God is forever and eternal. If we accept the Word which is also The Way (Christ) then we have sealed our destiny and protected ourselves in this life as we travel toward our ultimate destiny to live with Christ. The immortal words to that song says " oh I want to see him and look upon his face, there to live forever because of his saving grace, on the streets of glory, let me lift my voice, cares are past, home at last, ever to rejoice." Amen Saints! Don't let your flower wither in vain. Live for Christ and live.

24
POWER OF THE HOLY SPIRIT

For which cause we faint not; but though our outward man perish, yet the inward man is renewed day by day. **2 Corinthians 4:16**

Even though we are challenged within our flesh we are strengthened by and through The Holy Spirit. Paul said" I can do all things through Christ that strengthens me." Paul said also that " Every time I try to do good evil (temptations)are all around." "That that I would not I do and that that I would I do not." In spite of the discouragement along the way, the setbacks, the shortcomings, shortfalls and in general the failures we experience along life's journey, don't give up or give in. We are more than conquerors in Christ Jesus.

 The Holy Spirit is what renews us daily. The blessings of God start fresh everyday. Don't be discouraged by the compromise we see in the world. The Father is aware of your struggles and is allowing your deliverance and victory through your struggles that you survive if you don't quit.

Spiritual renewal comes from the transformation we experience when we don't conform to the ways of the world.

The scripture declares " I have never seen the righteous forsaken or his seed begging bread (looking for help). Jesus is our help and strength. We can have a relaxed mental attitude when we rest on the promises and assurances of God. Have faith and wait on him. He will surely perform it(whatever you need).

Trust in the Lord always and he will give you the desires of your heart. We have the power to wait through faith and trust in the Father Son and Holy Ghost. Amen Saints! Somebody needs this, will you share it please? God bless you with good measure, pressed down shaken together and running over.

25
EXHORTATION AND HELP

Walk in wisdom toward them that are without, redeeming the time. **Colossians 4:5**

Let your walk and your talk be tenderized and matured by the wisdom of God's word. Everyone that you encounter in life including those that you know will not be believers. Even some of the believers you know will not be spiritually mature enough to understand the struggles of the human species.

Motivational speakers are fine in seminars, business and places where worship is not the focus. I say that because in our world today many worship services have turned to motivational sessions rather than worship. I agree that no one wants to go to a humdrum worship service and a little spice can help the message but "The Word of God has all the motivation and spice we need to carry us through."

When the storm comes, a catchy phrase or what a preacher feels is an enlightenment won't help when the storms come up out of nowhere and you are all alone and that Pastor or Minister is nowhere to be found. That's why Timothy said " Study to show thyself approved unto God, a work men that needeth not be ashamed, rightly dividing (understanding) the truth, ye shall know (understand) the truth and the truth (word of God, God who is the truth) shall set you free.

Setting us free by the words means, we will be able to know what to do and make the necessary adjustments in our situations when the storms of life come rolling or raging in. In our culture, emotionalism can quickly take over if you don't watch your emotion and control them from being overrun with this motivational hype in some of our worship services in some of our largest churches today.

This is not a criticism but and observation of fact through the experience of having been in many of these services. Christ taught on the spoken word, fact, benefits, results, perseverance, long suffering, waiting, admonishments, hope, peace but most of all his grace through faith. Hype is not healing but healing through the word gives us all the help we need.

The word says " While I was yet speaking, the Lord heard me and delivered me from all of my fears (troubles or what I was going through)." Move away from Hype or emotionalism and receive the help you need from the Word. Jesus didn't use Hype, his words were simply " repent, forgive, love unconditionally and like he told Nicodemus " you must be born again" Amen Saints! Now if you think something needs to go viral as many of you put it, this does need to be read by both believers and non believers, especially those of us who are of the household of faith.

26
ACQUITTED AND FORGIVEN

(For he that wrought effectually in Peter to the apostleship of the circumcision, the same was mighty in me toward the Gentiles:) **Galatians 2:8**

Christ is the reason that I live and have breath. When we accept Christ we are crucified with him. We are not longer subject to hell and damnation, but have passed from death to life, no longer condemned but have life eternal. Our name is written in the Lambs Book of Life. Sealed unto the day of redemption.

Our name included in the book of the seven seals. No one can open this book but Christ. When it is finally opened your name is there only if you have confessed him as your personal Lord and Savior. When God told Noah to build an ark, because a great flood was coming. Noah didn't question God because there had not been rain and would appear to the natural mind, an exercise in futility. He did and he asked others for help in building the ark but they refused except for Noah's family.

In the end the rains came, and the people wanted entry on the ark for fear of their lives. That's how it's going to be in the final times when many will stand before the gates of Heaven and are denied entry because they thought it unnecessary to ask Christ to be Lord over their lives. Entry denied in Heaven but their entry will be approved for hell. Where will you rest eternally? Have you decided? This is the single most important decision we will make in our lives! Make the right choice and live! Make the wrong one and you have chosen to live in the pits of Hades forever.

It's not God's choice but yours. Jesus said in Revelation " I would that none should perish but all come into repentance. Trust in the Lord always and he will give you the desires of your heart. When we trust in Christ we know what to ask for and he supplies that need because you ask for what you want inside of his will. It is the Holy Spirit that you have decided to give control to and you follow its guidance. It's not easy, but when the Holy Spirit guides us you can say as the scripture declares, " it is no longer me who lives but the Christ who lives in me." He is now your Salvation, rock, refuge, strength, help, confidence, pathway, bread and everything you will ever need. Amen Saints! Great news for a chaotic world that we live in. Hope for yesterday, today and tomorrow until he comes. He's on his way back.

27
REPENTANCE AND FELLOWSHIP

Wash me throughly from mine iniquity, and cleanse me from my sin. **Psalms 51:2**

The blood of Christ is the only thing that can wash away our sins. After King David had committed the acts of Sin with Uriah's wife Bathsheba and the foiled plots that ultimately made it clear that he had to come clean with God even if he didn't with anyone else. David wrote the 51st Psalm in retrospect to his bloody hands and what he had been told by Nathan.

King David knew that if anyone could help him it had to be God. David loved God but he let his flesh get him into trouble. God had given the Holy Spirit to David and was the only one that could take it from him. In Old Testament times, the Lord would give or endow the Holy Ghost on who he willed or saw fit to lead and help the person. These people had favor with God and it was God's way to support the individual with his power.

This was a prayer of repentance from King David to God for what he had done. He acknowledged his sins but said that he was born in it and shaped in iniquity. He asked the Lord to clean him up by purging him with hyssop so that he would be clean and fit for continued service to God. He seems to want to make some kind of agreement or maybe a Covenant, when he said that if God would not take the Holy Spirit from him, he would point out to sinners their problems.

Our sins are between us and God. But God released King David from his fear of losing the Holy Spirit, but David had future problems with one of his sons named Absolom. Even though David sinned, tampering with the man of God is very dangerous and it has repercussions when you come up against God's called, chosen and sent servants. Like King David, we must acknowledge our sins and get back into fellowship with Christ. The good news for us New Testaments Christians, when Christ died all that believed on that name could never lose the Holy Spirit. John 3:16 is proof of that.

God does not go back on his word. Do you have a word? Have you either consciously or unconsciously gone back on your word with God or one of his children? Jesus is the washing agent that can wash away the guilt of your sins and purify you from your sin. 1 John 1:9 is proof of that, but is not your green light to keep sinning. When you keep sinning and keep utilizing this way out.

The other scripture comes into focus, Revelations 2:16-22. Those that I love I chasten (correct, rebuke and put my foot on them). Ask the children of Israel, who stayed in an in and out relationship with God until he had to ultimately send them into captivity in Babylon. Our flesh is the thing that causes us to fall out of fellowship but the Spirit keeps us in check when we let it guide us and keep us under its control of safety. Amen Saints!

28
JUSTICE AND FORGIVENESS

Casting down imaginations, and every high thing that exalteth itself against the knowledge of God, and bringing into captivity every thought to the obedience of Christ;

2 Corinthians 10:5

The imaginations of man shall be brought down but the ways of God shall be exalted. The man that thought he was doing what would bring him honor from his God by killing those innocent people in Manhattan New York, only had his plans foiled. Wrong will not ultimately prevail in the sight of God.

God is trying to get our attention to the fact of our falling away from the law and his covenants. The Father has given ample time for man to change his ways. Our attitude should be one of grateful appreciation for what the Father has done through his Son. Man has resorted to other means of refuge instead of the only one true and living God. God gave Moses the tablets that made it clear that he is a jealous God and he would have no other God's before him or taking his place, which is impossible.

This very day, we have this same attitude running rampant in our society, other God's that has caused man to falsely place his hope futilely in. Nothing that is sustainable was made for our benefit by any other God but Jehovah. The atrocious acts we have experienced will pale in respect to the greater atrocities that are coming our way.

Hurricanes Carla, Audrey, Rita, Katrina and Harvey just to name a few have momentarily got our attention. I say that because, man just believe that they were just storms during their season. Until man turns to total obedience to the Father, greater calamities will ensue. God's will is for man to succeed by service and obedience to God and to his fellow man, but man's greed is so out of control, that he doesn't realize the damage he's doing to God's creation and his people. The scripture declares " If my people who are called by my name, will humble themselves and pray and seek my face and turn from their sins, then will I hear from heaven, then I will heal their land (fix their circumstances)." Amen Saints!

29
ETERNAL SECURITY

Thus saith the Lord, thy Redeemer, the Holy One of Israel; I am the Lord thy God which teacheth thee to profit, which leadeth thee by the way that thou shouldest go. **Isaiah 48:17**

Jesus is the pathway that leads to life eternal. Have you ever been traveling in unfamiliar territory and had to stop and ask for directions? Have the directions that you got only led to further frustration? Have you been very near your destination but still stopped and asked for help only to find that the person you asked was lost also? Sometimes people want to truly help but they just don't know for sure the answer. That is why the Father sent the only answer that man can rely on and that is the Son Jesus.

The trouble with man is that his reliance usually is in his own intellect which fails him most of the time because his trust is in himself. The Bible and its written accounts inspired by God himself validates the way we should go. Jesus said" I am the way, the truth and the life, no man come through unto the Father except through the Son." Now this is the infallible evidence that there is no other that a man can be saved except through the Son.

Over the ages man has tried to validate that there has to be another way only to find out that there isn't. Look at other God's who tried to say that they were God's. Starting with the Egyptian God. It couldn't save Pharaoh or his son.

Allah is another one that is still in the grave. Buddha is another one, that is still in the grave. The only God that has, is and will do what he says is our God Jehovah. He said what was and is and was is to come and the what and is has already happened and is happening this very day.

The scriptures declare that by following the way Jesus, will benefit and profit the obedient. It couldn't be any plainer for man to see the way than what and who the Father sent in his Son Jesus Christ who hung bled and died for our benefit and the glory of his Father God. If you want to make it in this life and live eternally forever with God, then Jesus is the only way for you to accomplish that goal. Amen Saints!

30
DISCIPLINE

Now no chastening for the present seemeth to be joyous, but grievous: nevertheless afterward it yieldeth the peaceable fruit of righteousness unto them which are exercised thereby.

Hebrews 12:11

The discipline of the Lord may be painful but it results in peace and righteousness for those that overcome . Remember the fan belt, the lightening cord, the belt, the tree limb, the rope, the stick or the palm of the hand or whatever was convenient at the moment. In my day, my parents would discipline us with what was near them at the time. The fan belt hurt the worst and you really didn't like the idea of discipline.

The fact of the matter is that it didn't kill or harm me but it shaped me into the man I am today. Many people feel today however that kids today don't need the same type of discipline. Now look at the kids coming up today and those kids that grew up in the 60's and 70's and look at the difference. Jesus said" My son, reject not the chastening of the Lord." Beat him with a rod and he will not die" " Spare the rod and spoil the child." " Train up a child in the way he should go and when he is old (grown up, matured) he will not depart from it."

Have you not as an adult, reflected back on the correction you received from your parents while you were under their authority growing up? Those that rejected it, are either in prison or dead or didn't come to a good end. Discipline or correction originated from above and its intention was for man to be obedient to the Father and those who were in authority over them for their good. Our peace is directly tied to our obedience.

Now as an adult looking back you can see why discipline was so important. World order is tied to discipline but not tyranny or abuse. The Father doesn't abuse his children and corrects them with a hand of love. We have peace in our homes because of the spiritual correctness we learned growing up with mom and dad and sitting in those Sunday school classes that you didn't want to be in.

If your parents found out that you kept some of your money for cookies you bought from the corner store on your way home from church, that would have been another disciplinary moment. God's goodness and mercy is really what kept us then and keeps us now. Aren't you glad you know him and trust him and have introduced your family to him. Amen Saints!

31
RESPONSIBILITY

Let no man despise thy youth; but be thou an example of the believers, in word, in conversation, in charity, in spirit, in faith, in purity. **1 Timothy 4:12**

Just because you are young, don't let anyone take advantage of you. The enemy is looking around for someone to misuse. It really doesn't matter to him whether you are young, middle aged or a senior citizen. His goal is to inflict pain and discouragement. Inexperience can come in the form of knowledge or the lack of it and not necessarily age. David was young and inexperienced but God matured David according to his perfect Will. David grew in knowledge and stature through the will and favor of God. David allowed God to use him and followed God's instructions but his flesh got the best of him when he lost his focus the day he saw Bathsheba from the top of his palace bathing.

Everything that David believed was compromised when

he let his flesh take control of his spiritual senses. After all David was as we are flesh. When man allows his flesh to get in the way of him, every time, it doesn't end well. For David it came to blood on his hands and the murder of Uriah, the husband of Bathsheba. David did not actually kill him, but he ordered him to be placed in harm's way when his other plans failed.

When we try and live the way we profess, God steps in and helps us to maintain the right focus and attitude to overcome the inclinations to do wrong. Our nature is to do that which is not right in the sight of God, but that is where our faith we have through the Holy Spirit takes control and wheels us around evil deeds and thoughts. Let's face it, we are not strong willed in the natural enough to overcome these demonic attacks but the Holy Spirit is. So we have to Cleave unto that which is good and dispense with evil. The Holy Spirit is just that powerful and is ready to do work, if you will allow it and follow its guiding voice. Amen Saints.

32
OUR CALLING

Fight the good fight of faith, lay hold on eternal life, whereunto thou art also called, and hast professed a good profession before many witnesses. **1 Timothy 6:12**

We who are the called, lay hold, have faith and fight for that which you believe. Many people are fighting and causing all types of havoc, and really don't know why. The cause of Christ is a reality that you should fight for and understand why. The very essence of our being and destiny hangs in the balance.

Paul said that he lays hold on to that for which he is called into the fellowship of. Paul was speaking of his calling to do the work of God through Christ Jesus. We have that same calling on our lives, maybe not the same calling, but the work is the same. The work is to glorify the Father in heaven and to witness and disciple just as Paul did. Our work for the kingdom today is no less important than Paul's or any of the prophets of old.

We have to fight hard for this cause and maintain our faith, because the enemy is armed with every weapon in his arsenal to try and discourage and defeat us. Paul says in Philippians 4, "I can do all things through Christ that strengthens me." He also encouraged himself and us when he said" I count not myself to have apprehended (achieved, broken through) but this one thing I do, forgetting the things which are behind and reaching forth unto the things that are before or in front of me, I press toward the prize which is the high calling of Christ."

He is simply saying, he was not concerned so much about what he had failed at or didn't achieve. It was vitally important to keep his focus on the things in front of him and by faith he believed he would make it. That is what true faith is all about.

Where is your faith? Do you have any faith? Who or what is your faith anchored in? Well to put it like the words of that gospel song, my faith is anchored in the LORD!!! Great place to be secured and anchored. If you need an anchor that won't break or run in the middle of a fight, even when you may tuck your tail and run? Try Jesus today, right now! He will make your life brand new and he will take care of you, come unto Jesus while you have time! Amen Saints! Have a blessed evening and weekend.

33
SALVATION

For God so loved the world, that he gave his only begotten Son, that whosoever believeth in him should not perish, but have everlasting life.
John 3:16

Hearing and believing yields the faith we need to overcome the obstacles we have to face in this life. God has never gone back or not followed through on any promise that he has made through his word. When God says he is going to do something, he does it, even when we fall short on our part.

His love and his hands reaches us when we are in the depths of despair, indecision, confusion, arrogance, hatred and all of the emotions the enemy confronts us with. We have to know where our strength comes from and how to access his power and his promises. It is quite simple, this scripture tells us and gives us the roadmap to success in this life and the life hereafter.

The enemy wants you to believe that it's all tied up here. Who are you going to believe and trust? The creator that created everything, even the enemy or the cunning false promises of the devil? The truth of the matter is that nothing created is greater or can give you more than the creator. In everything and in all your weaknesses and your imaginary strengths, lean on him and his understanding and he will strengthen your heart (understanding) and direct the ways you should travel in this life that leads us to the next one.

God wills us in this life to be happy, safe, secure and he will provide everything we need to be so. Belief in the one that sent the Savior is the key to eternal security that unlocks the promises. We are the very essence and the object of his love and compassion for man and in spite of our continued failures to follow the written word to the letter which God knew was impossible for us, he sent the Son to save us, that is all that believe on this Christ. Amen Saints! . Somebody needs to hear this today! Help some lost soul today

34
A FRIEND AND A FATHER

Remember, and forget not, how thou provokedst the Lord thy God to wrath in the wilderness: from the day that thou didst depart out of the land of Egypt, until ye came unto this place, ye have been rebellious against the Lord.

Deuteronomy 9:7

Faithful is our God and merciful from everlasting to everlasting he is God. For those of you who may be going through something, he is your peace and the doorway that leads to understanding when we are perplexed, confused or in need of a friend who understands your situation.

He is a friend that will stick to you closer than a brother. His love is unconditional and not fair weather like many who say they love you but only fail you when you need them most. In a time of loss, controversy, despair, uncertainty and loneliness, he is the one who raises us up with his patience, forgiveness and long suffering.

Try him today and experience a change that Last your lifetime. Praise him and watch how his love overflows in your life. Amen Saints! Have a blessed day in the Lord.

35
SUCCESS

And whatsoever ye do in word or deed, do all in the name of the Lord Jesus, giving thanks to God and the Father by him. **Colossians 3:17**

All that we do in his name glorifies the Father, the Son and the Holy Spirit. The scripture declares that when we ask the Father for anything, it is granted when we ask it in Jesus name. Now that doesn't mean that if what we ask for it outside the will of God but in the name of Jesus, it will be done.

The key to asking successfully is asking inside his will and asking in his name. We shouldn't get angry or discouraged when we ask amiss or outside of his will, even though we ask in his name. We have to be fully in line with what the scripture says so that our requests or prayers will not be unsuccessful. When God says the only way to him is through the son.

He means just that. No deals, no shortcuts, no good deeds

or any other way will get you there but belief in the Son. So why put your eternal security at risk by following your own plan or what others speculate by what they call rational thinking. That's the problem, natural thought instead of Spiritual security that only comes by and through the Blood of Christ.

We are ambassadors or representatives of Christ as believers. All that we do and say should be fortified by his spirit which gives us the will and power to do and say what's right. Amen Saints.

36
ETERNAL VALUE

Hitherto have ye asked nothing in my name: ask, and ye shall receive, that your joy may be full. **John 16:24**

Experience my joy that I have for you by coming to me my son. Every good and every precious gift comes from above. The most powerful, beautiful, sustaining, everlasting, eternal and precious gift you could ever receive does not come from the hand of men but from God above.

If you were told that the land you were looking at purchasing had oil, gold, silver, copper, diamonds and untold cash buried on that land and it was an absolute fact. The only catch would be that you had to sell your soul to the devil in exchange for it. Many people either consciously or unconsciously have done just that.

The drive for the trappings of this world have driven men insane. The have and are looking to things for security rather than looking to and securing the safety and security of what the Father is giving us through the Son. In exchange for what the devil offers is work which ultimately ends in ruin, unrealized gain, because of the lie the enemy fooled you with.

Even if you gained the whole world and lost your soul. Did you really benefit from your work and futile efforts. Look at the benefits of the free gift of Salvation that you couldn't get by working for it. Peace, joy, eternal security, healing, deliverance, a true friend, an eternal home and all that you need while you live in the earth and most importantly in addition to Salvation, a father that watches over you and has you back and loves you unconditionally even when you turn away from him.

Wow! Simply amazing! All this because you put your trust in him! When we ask, seek and knock, the Father delivers through the Son. What an amazing life you can have, only if you put your trust in Jesus. Why not try Jesus for yourself today. Accept the Lord Christ today and he will take you to places your never dreamed of that are more precious and valuable than silver and gold. Amen Saints! Repost and share if you can! Jesus is the light of the world! An amazing relationship is awaiting your acceptance. Free to all, a healing stream, that flows from Calvary's mountain.

37
WISDOM AND PRAYER

Confess your faults one to another, and pray one for another, that ye may be healed. The effectual fervent prayer of a righteous man availeth much. **James 5:16**

Human wisdom is finite and is also fallible. This scripture is letting us know that it is alright to speak with one another about what may be troubling us. It is a good thing to honestly pray for one another and encourage one another. We have to also realize that God is the only one that can actually do something about and with our prayer requests. Our prayers are to be honestly directed to our Father in Heaven.

The prayers we pray generate real effect when they are prayed inside the will of God for his glory and our good. What is praying inside of his will? When we pray unselfishly and not ask for things to defeat our enemies. Let God handle that aspect of doing toward those that have wronged us. Praying inside his will is an obedient, loving, faithful, caring, delivering, forgiving, cleansing, healing and glorifying prayer toward God the Father.

Jesus said " First seek ye the kingdom of God and all of his righteousness and all these other things (what you are praying for) will be added unto you." Our healing comes from our first having ourselves cleansed by confession of our sins to the Father, by naming them according to 1 John 1:9. This scripture says " If we (you and me) confess our sins, to him (the Father) he (the Father) is faithful and just to forgive us of our sins and cleanse us from all unrighteousness."

Now when we do this, honestly through the spirit and not out of a ritualistic spirit, he hears us and our prayers have power and effect. We have to know and learn how to access the heavenly power we need as we journey through this world on our way home. Our home is with God in the New Jerusalem. While we are here, God has given us the keys to the kingdom so that we can experience the good and fat of the land here in the land of the living.

This is the will of God for our lives as his children who have accepted his invitation of Salvation through his Son who is our Savior, Jesus Christ our Lord. Amen Saints! Repost and share if you can. Go out and make it a great day. Come unto Jesus while you have time. Come unto Jesus, make up your mind. He will make your life brand new, for he will take care of you. Come unto Jesus, while you have time. Tomorrow might just be too late!

38
COMMUNICATION

But to do good and to communicate forget not: for with such sacrifices God is well pleased.
Hebrews 13:16

Communication is the vital key to understanding. The reason the Pharisees and many others didn't understand Christ is because there was a breakdown in communication on their part. When people only hear what they want to hear and not what needs to be heard, it causes a failure in understanding. Jesus always made sure his message was clear and concise and direct to the point.

His adversaries problem was that they were so hell bent on trying to trap him and prove their point, that they missed the point of his message. Jesus is the greatest communicator we will ever know. We need to ingest and take in the information before we try and respond to what is said to us. Many times we are responding before we get all of the information being communicated to us.

Communication is a two way street, not a one way street, either yours or mine. Usually, if we listen very close, the problem can be worked out or at least understood. We do good by really listening and then sharing our thoughts which promote good communication. Jesus said " As much as possible, try to live peacefully among men." So even Jesus knows that for many, communication was going to be hard but not impossible. Communication got so bad with the Pharisees that Jesus finally told them" This day the scriptures are seared in your hearing (your heart, your mind, your understanding)."

Jesus realized the fact that they didn't want to understand what he had been trying to communicate to them. So he simply by his providence, just sealed it in their minds. Many people we try to communicate with is of the same attitude toward us like those Pharisees. So we too like Jesus have to make a decision as to if they are getting the message without causing a problem for ourselves or them. Shake the dust off our shoes and move on like the scripture declares.

You ask the question. Do you understand? But you get no response. What are you to do with that? No communication is really a communication. When we try to effectively communicate to no avail, it's not our problem when the recipient ends up on the losing end. Sometimes you have to walk away as Jesus did with the Pharisees and finished the work that his father God sent him to do in the earth.

God knows our hearts and intents, so our attitudes are known of God. The word of God is sharper than a two edged sword and it cuts both ways and it can determine the hearts and intents of man. Amen Saints! What is your motive? God knows and you do too. Have a blessed day and rest of the week.

39
STEADFASTNESS AND STABILITY

Even a fool, when he holdeth his peace, is counted wise: and he that shutteth his lips is esteemed a man of understanding.

Proverbs 17:28

Fools rush in where angels dare to tread. Many people are considered to be unlearned only to be validated when they speak. People don't know what you know or don't know until you let them know by your words. True wisdom and knowledge comes from above. The knowledge that we get from the inspired word of God equips us for the journey that is set before us.

The Apostle Paul could speak 14 different languages and he had 7 degrees but he said " I count it all dung for the excellency that I found in Christ Jesus." Paul got his facts straight before he opened his mouth and was accused of being called a fool. Get the facts before you go to battle.

Even if someone calls you a fool or unlearned, you know the difference. Someone may accuse you of being this or that but you know the truth.

This is why you don't try and make sense out if nonsense. Proverbs says "A word to the wise is sufficient." You know what you know and learn to be satisfied with that. Even a fool knows when to keep quiet and so should we. God's children are not fools even though the world thinks so. Keep your peace and don't give place to the devil.

They tried to say that Jesus wasn't the Christ when he told them that he was. People will try and disclaim your claims that you make that you have been changed. Some will challenge you as they did Christ, but he was still and is still who he said he is and you are too. Ride on king Jesus, no man can hinder you or his children!Amen Saints! Have a blessed day and rest of the week.

40
DELIVERANCE HEALING AND RESTORATION

Come unto me, all ye that labour and are heavy laden, and I will give you rest. **Matthew 11:28**

Jesus is our anchor and our resting place from our troubles. When we see the word that says "come" in the Bible from Jesus. He is saying to us, to yield your life first over to him and then allow him to fix your problems.

The blood you received from you yielding or allowing him to come in gives him the authority to began to help you navigate through your issues you face and will face on life's journey. Notice the scripture tells us to come to him, not your neighbor, your best friend, your confidant, your parents or even your Pastor. He says come to him. Restoration and deliverance, healing and all that you need can only come from and through him.

We don't have to carry all of the weights we carry. The enemy tries to make us believe we are all alone, but we are not, God is with us every step of the way, even when we are in our darkest place or places. Psalms 23 says with a shout" yea though I walk through the valley and the shadow of death (trouble) thou art with me." So if we come to him with our troubles, he will eventually give us rest or peace, deliverance, restoration that we need. Give all of your worries over to him, he can and wants to handle them and he will. God will not go back on his promises which is his word. Amen Saints!

41
GUIDANCE

A man's heart deviseth his way: but the Lord directeth his steps. **Proverbs 16:9**

We can stand on the mountain only after God shows us how to climb it. In this life we plan for many things. We plot out the course for ourselves and our children. We go to school, get educated in what we believe will help us grow financially, we make sure our children get a good education, we get a home for our families, we buy the transportation we need to get us from place to place, we plan for the families vacation, we look around for a good church to attend.

So we basically try to do what we feel is right in our own mind. The failure behind it all many times is that we fail to let God lead us all the way. The Bible says" The steps of a good man are ordered by the Lord." We can sometimes make logical decisions but when it comes to the real deal, God is the one who should influence and steer us into the proper placement of our decisions.

Have you ever ordered something in a restaurant and when you got your food it wasn't done to your satisfaction. What did you do? They did it over or you left the restaurant because you weren't satisfied with them not following your instructions. We make plans but God allows for our destination to get there if we follow his plan and not ours.

Our journey here can be be sweet if we are obedient and follow his instructions. The truth about the matter is simply that God gives us freedom of choice, are you making the right choices? When we choose to follow him, you have made the right choice and you are traveling on the right street that is called straight. Amen Saints! Have a blessed day!

42
OBEDIENCE AND SAFETY

He that dwelleth in the secret place of the most High shall abide under the shadow of the Almighty. **Psalms 91:1**

We are safe in the shelter of his all encompassing shadow. The shadow of God is simply his covering of our lives by the power of his word through the blood of his Son. Those of us who live by the obedience of his commands shall be benefitted by the promises of his provision.

We have to know that all of the military, police, fire, coast guard and any man provided safety mechanism is not stronger or more protective than the arm and power of the Almighty. The shelter and rest we find in the most high God can only be accessed through our relationship with the Holy Spirit.

The Holy Spirit is the guide that warns us of oncoming danger and leads us in the direction we must go. You can be a Christian believer and because of your choices fall into the predatory traps of the devil. That's why the scriptures say" those whose life is governed by their actions and following the instructions of the most high God, will reap the benefits of an obedient life under the direction of the most high God."

So if I live to Christ, no matter what may come my way, I know that my life is in his hands and God will prevail for his and my good. Amen Saints! . Have a blessed day!

43
FAITHFULNESS

Know therefore that the Lord thy God, he is God, the faithful God, which keepeth covenant and mercy with them that love him and keep his commandments to a thousand generations;

Deuteronomy 7:9

First there is only one true and living God! There is also no greater or more faithful God than him. The scripture declares him to be faithful to a thousand years. This just simply means that his blessings are perpetual or never ending. His blessings start fresh and new everyday.

Are we as faithful to him as he is to us? No. Beachside he is perfect and we are imperfect and many times impossible. His authority and providence reached in all directions, he is always moving forward but many times have to reach back to rescue and redeem us.

When we trust him, he covers our families for generations to come and gives us the capacity to love, forgive, rebuke and reprove with an unconditional love like him. Seek him while he may be found. We can trust him when we can't trust ourselves.

44
TRANSFORMATION

And be not conformed to this world: but be ye transformed by the renewing of your mind, that ye may prove what is that good, and acceptable, and perfect, will of God. **Romans 12:2**

Don't act like the world that we live in but transform yourselves into the image of God. The world is filled with tricks, gimmicks, foolery, compulsions, intimations, masks and all of the things that are not life giving according to the spirit. The spirits rule but which spirit is ruling you? Families fighting each other over nonsense, brothers and sisters in confusions against each other, neighbors think they are more than you and live in the same neighborhood.

The enemy is the architect behind all of this worldly mess. The Bible constantly reminds us the spiritual mind transformation needed to understand and free ourselves from the perils of this world. Transformation means to change from how and what you think about and focus in on the main thing of why God brought you here. What is that you might ask?

Focus on God and service to him and our fellowship with him and man. To love each other with the unfailing love of Christ that was poured out for us at Calvary regardless of our sins and trespasses against a perfect sacrifice sent from the Father to save his creation. The problem with all of us to a great extent is that we have forgotten what it means to forgive and we remember the sacrifice of God forgiveness through the Son Jesus.

I hear you say, no I have not forgot what Christ did and I have not forgot what you did me either, whether it's brother, father, sister, mother, neighbor, friend, stranger or whoever. The simple fact is that Christ forgave and forgot what we did and had given us the power through the blood spilled on Calvary to do the same. Listen to me! Are you listening? Your life (put your name there) will never amount to what God intended for it to be until you let go of the past and what you have been mad about and who you are mad with.

Give your cares, concerns, anger, hate, lies, problems and all of the shackles that have been holding you down all of your life and let Jesus Christ our Lord free you from stress and guilt and fly like an eagle and see and experience what God has planned for you in this generation where you are and the blessings of the generations to come.

Love your God, family and friends with the unconditional love God has freely given you in this world and the one to come. Share this everybody with your immediate family, especially your siblings and this close to you and who use to be close to you. Amen Saints! . Love is an action word, do it today, for tomorrow just might be too late. A message from God's Heaven. Wrote this while sitting and feeding my Father-n-Law and watching a football game with my Father-n-Law who is to me like a father. Peace be still and watch God move that mountain. I know what he has, is and going to do according to our faith.

45
PROTECTION AND DISCERNMENT

Put on the whole armour of God, that ye may be able to stand against the wiles of the devil.

Ephesians 6:11

The whole armor is what prevents the devil from slipping through a door left open. The enemy doesn't care how he gets in, he just wants an entry point to create havoc in our lives. The word of God is our protection and promise that God would stand with us and catch the fiery darts of the devil. We cannot know all of the cunning tricks of the devil, we can't recognize all of his disguises but God knows where he is and what his moves are. That's why it's important for us to wear all of God's provision of protection.

When we realize the fact that the enemy may come in the form of your friend, but God's armor will reveal to you whether he is really a friend or a foe. This armor is for your protection as well as your spiritual knowledge so that you can discern what is God's will for your life and why as believers we have to go through divers temptations sometimes for our good and our growth. The recent storm named Harvey was sent for a number of reasons. All of which we may never know, but God was revealing to you his power and letting us know that we can't depend on man but we can defend on the creator.

Man has strayed to far from God and has become arrogant, and God is not satisfied with man's attitude. After all God has done to place man in the positions that he's in. Man now believes that he is the brains behind his successes and that is his problem. He believes that he doesn't need the whole armor or perhaps none of it because he is lifted up in foolish pride. God has a way of showing us who is still in charge. Man is still trying to figure out this universe, but all he has to do is to follow God's directions.

When Israel followed God's plan, they did well until they lost focus on God and began to focus on themselves and what they wanted. The Commandments was the whole armor God was talking about but they didn't want to follow them and as a result they experienced God's wrath. Now in our dispensation of time, the whole armor is from Genesis to Revelation. Somebody missed the message of storm Harvey and now the Lord has awakened Jose who might be the next storm.

What is it going to take before man looks up and consult God for his directions. Consult God and live or continue in disobedience and run the risk of destruction. Put on the whole uniform of God and be a spiritual force to be reckoned with in the land of the living or while you are on your way to the land of the living. This earth is where man dies and heaven is where he lives forever. You make the call. Amen Saints! Pray everyone made it alright through the storm in Texas and those that will come.

46
LOVE AND FORGIVENESS

And now abideth faith, hope, charity, these three; but the greatest of these is charity.
1 Corinthians 13:13

Everything that man does seems to be right in his own eyes, but God knows your heart(your motives). The darkness of the clouds in this picture illustrates the evil in man that only God can see straight through. Many times we say one thing but our motives are far from what we are projecting.

The word of God is sharper than a two edged sword and it cuts to the dividing asunder of the bones, joints and marrow and it is a determiner of the hearts and intents of a man. This is the power of the word of God who is God himself. How can you not know that you can't out think or out maneuver God. Who has declared the power and benefit of God's word to our government officials? Are they exempt from God's reprisal? His wrath? His correction ? No they are not! They are mere men who have lost their way in terms of their responsibility to God's people.

Pride cometh before the fall. Just as we are to respect the civil laws of government put in place by God, our leadership in government are to abide by the ordinances of God's words. On the other hand we as Christians have a responsibility to pray for and ask God to help our leaders and bless their minds and actions. But the distinction is that when the actions of our leaders are oppressive and persecutory to God's children, someone is going to have to pay the price for that evil. Now the scripture tells us that we should pray for them persecute you and do harm to you for his sake(because you use the power of his words) you bless them and don't curse them or wish harm for them) it's like putting heaps of coal (his punishment) on them.

It is he(God) that exacts the punishments on them, not us. We have to follow the directions if we want to get it right. "Vengeance is mine says the Lord, I will repay." This is the charity part of the scripture that he talks about that is the greatest gift of the three, faith, hope and charity(love is the same as charity). I know it's hard when you see a President and a congress, local and state officials that support what we see, but God is the one who makes all wrong right, every crooked thing straight.

We just have to do our part and let God do the rest! He will do what he said. The question is, will you do what you say you will do and do what you promised God you said you would do? Amen Saints! The storm is not over yet, but the sender of the storms of life knows exactly where you are and what you are thinking to do and what you will actually do no matter what you are saying. You can't fool the Father! Do right and get your blessings no matter what your enemy does or try to do! Have a blessed and safe day wherever in the world you are.

47
A UNIVERSAL INVITATION

Behold, I stand at the door, and knock: if any man hear my voice, and open the door, I will come in to him, and will sup with him, and he with me. **Revelations 3:20**

This is a personal and Royal invitation to you. How many times have you received an invitation from someone and you put it aside. It said you must RSVP, but you didn't. Sometimes you just went and were allowed to get in and sometimes you went only to find that your name was not on the list. You were told that entrance was by your RSVP that you failed to pay attention to. This is one such RSVP that you should not overlook, set aside, say I will get to it later.

This invitation has eternal benefits and ramifications. This information is what you have been waiting for with great anticipation of its worth. This invitation is worth more than all the gold at Fort Knox, it's more powerful than all of the worlds atomic and nuclear weapons, more devastating than the floods of Noah's day. Don't miss your opportunity to open up the door and let him in when he knocks on the door of your conscious mind.

It's too important to let someone or something divert your attention from this.

This door is in heaven and he's waiting to open it to you and welcome you home when it's your time. Jesus himself is the one knocking at the door of your mind, he is not going to send nobody but himself, he makes the statement and issues the benefits. He says he will come in and and sit and eat with you and be your friend (your protection, safety, assurance, lifeboat, seal, healer, deliverer and all that you need). But you have to hear him when he knocks and you have to take the action of opening up the door to let him in.

Don't do him like you do some of your friends when they drop by unannounced, look through the peephole in your door and see them and act like you're not home. You better receive him so you can get home! This is not your home.

We have a storm here in Texas and it may be headed your way, the weather people named it Harvey, but God is really speaking to us through this storm. Are you listening? Amen Saints! Have a safe and blessed day! The song says" I've been through the storm and rain, but I made it." We are gonna make it this time and the next time until he calls you or comes to get us, if you answered your door when he knocked.

48
CONFIDENCE

Have not I commanded thee? Be strong and of a good courage; be not afraid, neither be thou dismayed: for the Lord thy God is with thee whithersoever thou goest. **Joshua 1:9**

The confidence you need comes from the spirit of God within us. Man often times listen to the wrong people that gives him a false sense of things. Confidence is something that is built over time and not given. A child's gains his confidence to walk with the support of someone showing and helping them make their first few baby steps.

After falling a few times, pulling up on the coffee table, stumbling as they try to walk toward you on their own, they finally do it. How happy they are and you too but now they get into everything. Right? Now fear shakes our confidence, it puts a halt on your will to go forward. The Lord is our confidence.

The scripture declares " He did not give us a spirit of fear or timidity (lack of confidence) but a spirit of love, power(confidence) and a sound mind." We can overcome our fears by leaning on the spirit and not the advice of others. Jesus is all the strength and courage we need to forge forward. With the Lord behind us we can move ahead with the confidence and power we need to get things done for the kingdom of the living God.

If God be for us who can be against us. We are more than conquerors in him. Be strong in the Lord and the power of his might. I can do all things through Christ that strengthens me. Spiritual strength gives us courage and courage gives us power and power comes from the spirit which produces patience which allows us to exemplify the fruits of the spirit.

All of our help cometh from the Lord. Lean on him and trust him and watch your life soar. We get better each day and bitterness cannot take hold of us for long. Amen Saints. Have a blessed day and week.

49
BOLDNESS AND INTEGRITY

He keepeth the paths of judgment, and preserveth the way of his saints. **Proverbs 2:8**

The storms may rise and so does the waters, but he is faithful to see us through. How many times you thought in your mind, well this is it. Let me get things in order, my time is running out. Only to receive a breakthrough and a change order of your circumstances from God. The enemy oftentimes paints very bleak picture that he keeps in front of us when we take our eyes off God and focus on our problems or our circumstances.

I know for me that God is my hiding place, my shelter in a time of storm. The scripture says He watches over them that are faithful to him." In other words, he keeps his wings of protection over us. We have to wear and execute our faith in him through all things, no matter how hard pressed it can get. Don't throw in the towel so quick. Stand on his word and fight. God is like a tag team member, when he touches you on the shoulder, it's his time in the ring to fight the enemy. Believe me, he will deliver the knockout blow to your enemies. He said "I will fight your battles, no matter what they are and how many they are." He also said "Whatever you need me to be for you I am." If you need him to be a healer, deliverer, conqueror, peace, a table in the presence of your enemies, shelter, the water that quenches your soul, let him be that, he'll do it. I know he will, because he promised in his word. He is not like us, he will not go back on his word. Will you try him today? Amen Saints! Have a blessed day today and all week.

50
HOPE

Those things, which ye have both learned, and received, and heard, and seen in me, do: and the God of peace shall be with you.

Philippians 4:9

You have heard that it takes a whole village to educate a child. Who helped the village? What is happening in this world today? The disconnection of mankind, the hatred between the races, the discord in our leadership, the lack of love in the family, the disparity in opportunity, the tricks of the enemy, unforgivable hearts and deliberate attacks on mankind.

These are not the acts that the Father intended for his creation. Every man does right in his own eyes but that is what has caused the ills we see in our society today. In order for man to survive and thrive the way God intends, he has to follow the will and direction of the Almighty. This scripture says it plainly. What we have seen, heard and learned in Christ, we are to put that in practice. The benefits are that the God of peace will be with us. Philippians 4:9.

It doesn't really matter about the color of your skin, what matters is who is your God? Some want you to believe that he is the color of their skin, therefore they are his original people. The Bible does not teach prejudice but it does teach about praise and who praise should be raised toward and why. The issue of color will not be raised or important when we get to Heaven. Immortality does not reason with mortality. When we get to Heaven our thoughts that we have here won't be the reality we have in eternity.

The Bible says we shall see him just as he is. So what color you may have thought he was when you were mortals won't make a difference when we meet him face to face. That's why the Bible records that God is a spirit and they that worship him must worship him in spirit and in truth. This truth is sealed in the infallible records left in his word.

This is in what he has taught, shown and allowed you to see through the spirit. Now this is what you should put into practice so that you can realize the benefits of him and his peace being with you. Strife and discord will always be in this world but you can have peace when you follow him, who is your strength and the word. Amen Saints! Have a wonderfully blessed day.

51
ENCOURAGEMENT

Those things, which ye have both learned, and received, and heard, and seen in me, do: and the God of peace shall be with you.

Philippians 4:9

In the test to keep our minds on things above. The Apostle Paul said "Let this mind be also in you that is in Christ Jesus." In order to put into daily practice those things that we have seen, heard and learned from Christ, we have to think like him and operate in the spirit even though we are in the world.

Christ said " Even though we (the believers) are in the world, be not apart of it or don't buy into what world is doing. Many people think they can do a part of the world and do a part of Jesus when it is convenient. That is what causes The chasm between this world and our Kingdom Connection.

52
INTERVENTION

Who is a wise man and endued with knowledge among you? let him shew out of a good conversation his works with meekness of wisdom. **James 3:13**

I am speaking to all of the world whom I alone created! Are you listening? The Bible says" A word to the wise is sufficient." There are so many indications that God is and has been trying to get our attention. A couple of weeks ago, tragedy stuck America in Charlottesville, West Virginia, the cover has been taken off of our racial divide on every level,

Once again we see out in the open, bigotry, prejudice and inhumanity between the races. The human race began in the garden of Eden with the fall of Adam. Look at the fall of man that started way back then. If man could solve these issues then Jesus would not have had to come. He came to bring back together his creation that was separated from him. Man because of his flawed nature and character keeps bigotry, racial injustice and race separation afloat.

Look at what God spoke about today in Barcelona Spain. This was an attack on man, irrespective of race. God is not prejudiced in terms of his creation. He is however against those who oppose his wisdom. God's wisdom directs us in a human way to filter goodness and mercy toward one another irrespective of race, ethnicity and national origin. Man has caused the debacle between the races, not God. This is a word that needs to go viral as our world calls it.

It appears that the nations values all over this world are steeped in selfish and human conceits. From the highest level of government to The homelessness on our streets, bigotry and inhumanity reigns. Now if government and the poor cannot get it together mainly because neither will look up and concede that the solution is only found in God. Now until this nation, we call the home of the free and the land of the brave, look up and ask God for his divine help, you can bank on it that things will get increasingly worse.

This applies to all nations, not just America. None can bring peace, calm, sensibility and human care like our creator. Until we cry out to the Father like Israel did in their crisis, we will go on wondering like Israel did in the wilderness. The Saints of God need to individually and collectively go down in prayer and stay there until heaven answers and shows us what to do.

Man does not have the right attitude to solve this one, the righteous answer is waiting on our cry and will be sent from above. The answer once lived among us and is now seated at the right side of the Father who makes intercession for us. Amen Saints! . The nations needs to see this and share. Have a blessed day people of God and all who wish to become a part of his royal family.

53
COMMISSION AND INSTRUCTION

Teach me to do thy will; for thou art my God: thy spirit is good; lead me into the land of uprightness. **Psalm 143:10**

In order for God to lead us we have to be willing to follow. The writer said" I will follow you, wherever you lead me." He was referencing following God. The scripture asked the question. Who will go for us? The servant answered and said" Here I am Lord! Send me!" God has a mission for our lives, but he has the road map and directions for us to follow. Following God has no shortcuts or back alley ways to cut through.

His plan is perfect and the steps we take are sure steps sent from above. They are not designed to hamper or fool us. They are there to carry us along the pathway he has chosen for us. Many times as we are directed, the enemy will send something or someone to get in your way, to slow you down, to stop your momentum.

The Holy Spirit is the guide within us if we have accepted Christ. This guide leads us to all truth and the success that God has planned for us long ago. When we study and apply the truths of his words, we can be assured that he will guide our feet(mind) so that we travel this life on level ground, even though we go through our own ups and downs, still tarring on level ground. How? You might ask? The scripture says" All things works to the good of them who love God and are the called according to his purpose."

Make it a habit to follow God, even when you may be experiencing travail, he is at that point working things out for your good, believe it or not. It's your call. Amen Saints! Have a wonderful day and bless his Holy name.

54
CHARACTER

And we know that all things work together for good to them that love God, to them who are the called according to his purpose.

Romans 8:28

God works all things to benefit us no matter how they may appear to us. Now, the only way you can know this, is first you have to know God. To know him you have to understand a few things about his nature and his character. Both of these attributes of God are totally opposite of ours in the embodiment of the Almighty.

 He does what he says and he says only what is in his nature and character he will do. He is not like man, man will tell you one thing, knowing full well that he hasn't the nature and character nor intent to follow through on what he promises. Man has a flawed nature and character from the start as a child and it fully develops over his life. That's what David was saying as his excuse when he penned the 51st Psalm.

"In sin did my mother conceive me." He was saying that he couldn't help himself because of the curse of his flesh, that dates back to Adam in the garden of Eden. Now, we may be born with that kind of flesh but Christ dispelled that when he shed his blood at Calvary. Paul said" In my flesh dwells no good thing." "Every time I try to do good evil is all around. " was it the evil in Paul or the evil around him or both? Now matter his reasoning or yours or mine, the blood of Christ made a way for us to escape the evil that had us destined for hell.

Now what you may be dealing with may be the trials of your faith, so that God can see how for real your statements of faith really are. This could also be how God strengthens you for the battlefields you will be facing ahead. Now matter what you may see or be experiencing, remember your Savior lives and he lives in you, to protect, lead and guide you, if you follow his directions. Making pancakes are easy even if you don't know how to cook. All you have to do is follow the directions on the box. God's directions are in the book(The Holy Bible) Not the revised editions, but the ones that were wrote on the scrolls and inspired by the power of God through the Holy Spirit. Many people want to question the King James Version.

Man could not interpret with the accuracy and power in this collection of infallible truths. It had to be the Trinity of power from Heaven imprinting the thoughts of the Almighty in the mind of the conveyor of The Words words. So in conclusion, what he has done, is doing and will do in your life is all for your benefit and the benefit of your testimony to others, which is your reasonable service. Amen Saints! Have a blessed day, because you have not seen this day before and you will never see it again. God does not have to repeat, he is too busy bringing you forward.

55
PATIENCE

I wait for the Lord, my soul doth wait, and in his word do I hope. **Psalm 130:5**

Them that wait(trust, depend, rely and have faith) shall renew their strength. In the context of this scripture, waiting means to have trust and patience because we know that the Lord will make a way and come through for us that believe as he always does. The security and assurance of his promises allows the believer to have confidence in his word.

Little children have great confidence in what their parents say or promise them. They are very disappointed when we don't make good on our promises or commitment to them. The child who has been waiting for dad to pick him up says to a parent that offers him a ride. No thank you, my dad said for me to wait here for him until he gets here to get me. It's getting a little late, you better let us give you a lift, just a that moment, dad shows up and the kid says, I told you that he would get here to get me.

Jesus is one who we can wait on with that same childlike confidence and patience. Jesus will always do what he says and will never go back on his promises. Can Jesus trust what we commit to him? The disappointment we feel when our prayers are not answered in what we feel are a timely manner is the same feeling that God feels when we don't follow through on what we commit or promise him. Commitments and promises are not to be taken lightly when we spiritually commit or make a vow with the Lord.

It's better to not make one than to make one and break it. Imagine the hurt you would feel if you accepted Christ and when he gets back on the second advent, he doesn't take you back with him. You would probably be screaming to the top of your voice " but you promised me." We don't have to worry or agonize over that, because he will not go back on his promises, because our faith is built on his promises of his word.

Now then you can see from this illustration how important having a word is and how important trust is. Can Jesus trust you and believe on your promises? Let's start today living the life we declare in our faith. No matter how hard it gets, live what you say and say what you live. We can't have it both ways! Living according to the world's standards when it's convenient and God's standards when we fall into trouble. We will have to trust him in all things if we say we are his. Amen Saints! Somebody needs to hear this!

56
LOVE IN ACTION

In whom we have redemption through his blood, the forgiveness of sins, according to the riches of his grace; **Ephesians 1:7**

With the blood of his Son, he freed us from the bondage of sin. Because of God's great and passionate love for us, he allowed the death of his son to bring us the grace and forgiveness required for us to escape the penalty of death. His love is unconditional and we as Christians should have this same type of love toward one another.

This was what he was driving us to embrace when he said "I bring to you a new commandment that ye love one another as I have loved the church." The church is not the building that we worship in but the Holy Spirit he endowed us with at the moment of our personal salvation through Christ Jesus. Loving us is not easy, but he does. Loving people is not easy but you can through the spirit.

Love is an action word, not just talk. When Jesus went to the cross, it was an action, not talk, thought he did mention along the way that things would occur but he had overcome those things. So then the take away from this should be that as Christ has looked past our misdeeds and ministered to our needs, we should be able to do the same toward each other. You can say I am sorry even if you were not at fault.

That's what Jesus did when he went to the cross to pay with his life for a wrong that he didn't commit, because of his awesome love, mercy and his grace. The truth is that we want to be forgiven and many times we don't want to forgive.

We say something like " I will forgive you but I won't forget it." Jesus did both, forgave and forgot, that's what going to the cross was all about. If you haven't forgotten? Have you really forgiven. That is how the devil keeps his wedge in our relationships and some marriages. Forgive and it shall be forgiven you. Give your relationships and marriages a chance, forgive, forget and let God remove the wedge from your lives and homes. Jesus died to do that for us, so accept this mandate and live a healthy life. Amen Saints!

57
CHOICES AND PERSECUTIONS

For do I now persuade men, or God? or do I seek to please men? for if I yet pleased men, I should not be the servant of Christ.

Galatians 1:10

The persuasion of God leads to the light. Man has been persuaded and will be swayed by many things in this life. The value of reason is a volitional choice and can lead us to the traps of the enemy or the safety of Christ. The Apostle Paul made the choice when he was Saul, by reason of choice, to persecute the Christians he found in the way.

The way was Christ and he by choice fought the way, which was the choice of Christians following Christ in that day as well as those who fight the church in our day by choice. Choices can be devastating and crippling. What choices have you made that have got you caught up or entangled in something that only God could bring you through? Remember you said,"I can control this, I can quit when I get ready!" It was not until God decided to help Saul that his choice to persecute the church became his commission and mission to promote the church.

If The Lord had not blinded Saul on his way to do evil, he never would have gained his sight to see the evil he had been found. If we never come to Christ we also will never see what the Lord has for us to do as a child of the king and the work of a kingdom builder. If Saul had never followed what the Lord told him to do, he would still have been blind and could not do what he was traveling to do in Damascus. What are you traveling to do? What is your mission or commission in this life? Have you tried your hands at God's work or are you still trying to do things your way? How is your way working out for you? Make a u-turn and come back to him or turn right and go straight to him.

It's your call but he waiting on you to make the right decision. Saul's decision to serve men or the Sanhedrin Council of men, turned out to be his err and his folly, until God lovingly changed his course. Let Christ change your course and stop trying to please yourself and others. Become Christ's servant and let him show you the way, he knows the way because he is the way, the truth and the life. After Saul's conversion he became a beacon of light for the cause of Christ. He said that whatever things he had accomplished, he counted it all rubbish or trash in comparison to the excellency he found in Christ.

Paul was a changed man, with a changed heart, a changed mission and a changed life with a changed destination and a place in heaven. Why not serve instead of wanting to be served. Confess Christ as your personal Lord and Savior if you haven't already and secure your seat at the supper table with Christ. The Father has sent you an invitation. Have you accepted it yet? Do it today! Paul said" For I Am persuaded that nothing can ever separate us from the love of God." That's a promise for all who place their trust in Christ. Amen Saints!

58
PROMISES

All that the Father giveth me shall come to me; and him that cometh to me I will in no wise cast out. **John 6:37**

Everyone that the Father gives to me will come and I will receive them. The Son knew before we did all who would receive his offer of Salvation. He is ready for us to stretch our hands toward him like a little child just learning how to walk. He will guide us and make our uncertainties certain.

He will strengthen our weak and wobbly legs so that we can make strong and sure steps like the little child who can now not only stand but run to his parents. Oh the joy in the heart and eyes of the Father when he sees the maturity of his children. He will never turn away from us and will always be there to catch us when we fall.

There to help us up again and place us on the right track. We are special to him and his will is to see us prosper in the spirit as well as in our natural lives. The only way we can receive this guidance is by first coming to him and then living in obedience. He is our king and we as his children are the objects of his love. Amen Saints! Have a blessed day and a blessed Communion Sunday on tomorrow.

59
ASSURANCE

Who shall separate us from the love of Christ? shall tribulation, or distress, or persecution, or famine, or nakedness, or peril, or sword?

Romans 8:35

Once in Christ never out, praise God Saints. Just as Jesus died once and his act of Love that brought us Salvation was for once and forever. He does not have to die over and over spilling his blood again and again for our Salvation. Once was all that was required of his Father God to reconcile us and make peace with God and secure our Heavenly eternal destination.

Once is all that it takes for us to accept Christ as our personal Savior and we are forever accepted in the royal family of God and our eternal destination is set and can never be revoked. This is the assurance we have from our covenant God, who follows through on his word.

Now then as the scripture asked. Can anything separate us from the love of Christ? The answer is emphatically no!

Once we established relationship with Christ is seals us from separation. Nothing you can do can break this seal of promise. Now we can go through faith challenges but remain unseparated.

We can experience difficulty because of disobedience but remain unseparated. The issues of life and everyday living can happen but we remain connected to our God and his ultimate protection during and after the storms of life. Rest assured that nothing can separate us or tear us apart once we are connected by the blood. Amen Saints! Now this is one that really needs to be shared. Have a remarkably wonderful day.

60
CHOICES

The Lord is not slack concerning his promise, as some men count slackness; but is longsuffering to us-ward, not willing that any should perish, but that all should come to repentance. **2 Peter 3:9**

The door to repentance is always open and available for us to walk through. Don't take the Lord's patience as though he is being neglectful regarding his promises. He wants to make sure that everyone that wills has ample chances to come out of the rain(trouble in the world of sin). The Lord knows that all who does not follow his plan will ultimately be destroyed or sent to eternal damnation in the lake of fire.

Ask the rich man about the great chasm between his place of torment and the blessings of Lazarus dwelling with God. The Lord knows that a life in eternity without him is no place for us. So it is his will to allow us a chance to make the right choice of our eternal destination. The

Father's will that none be lost, is still a choice that has to be personally made by each of us.

Don't get so busy trying to achieve the trappings of this world that we lose sight of the main reason for our existence. We were bought with a price and set apart for his glory. When we accept the fact that it is only through the blood that we are set apart and choose him as our Lord and Savior, only then are we ready to understand our part we play in this life and the one to come.

We shouldn't pay so much attention to what the world thinks in relation to the Father. How the world thinks and how God thinks are worlds apart. If we don't get it right by making him our choice, we won't like the eternal dwelling place down under and I am not talking about Australia, the land down under. We should aspire to be patient and longsuffering just as he is one toward another. Our choice has eternal ramifications. Amen Saints! Have a blessed evening and week.

61
THE NARROW GATE

For I know the thoughts that I think toward you, saith the Lord, thoughts of peace, and not of evil, to give you an expected end. **Jeremiah 29:11**

There's only one road that leads to life. There are many roads to choose from on the journey we call life. It's not like Dorothy, toto and her friends that happen to find the city of Oz. Like Dorothy, she had to find someone that could get her back home to Kansas. Our home is heaven and the only one that can take us there, and is waiting with open arms to lead you to a blessed life here and then to the place prepared for you in heaven,

Our eternal home with God. This one's name is Jesus, The Lamb of God and The Lion of Judah. Along life's highway, there are many exits that lead to many places, but the exit that leads to him is a narrow gate in the road that leads to the kingdom. There is another road or exit that leads to destruction and the sad commentary is that, this is the road that many choose to travel to their doom. All that placed the blood over the door post like God told Moses to tell them were passed by when death's angel came through.

Likewise in our journey, the blood is the only thing that allows us to escape death that leads to life eternal. His ways and thoughts are not ours, but the good news is that he has great plans for all who accept what he has done through Jesus Christ. So accepting the blood is mandatory to access eternal rewards. Jeremiah 29:11 spells it all out. He basically says that his thoughts are directed towards all who accept the son. He knows the plans he has for us, peace of mind and not evil. Our end ultimately through Christ is a heavenly destination if the kind of peace we won't really understand until we get home.

When we get home all of our worries will be over. When we get home all of the issues of life will have ended. When we get home the Sun will shine forever and there will be no need if the Sun, because The radiance of God will be all the light we need. So why not secure your destiny and inheritance today.

Accept Jesus if you haven't already and be born again, like he told Nicodemus in answers to the question he asked Jesus. Nicodemus asked Jesus" What must I do to inherit eternal life?" In other words " What must I do to go to heaven, when I die and leave this place?" Jesus told him" don't be amazed or shocked by what I am about to tell you, you must be born again." Jesus was saying that you must have a spiritual birth, not another biological birth like Nicodemus surmised, which was an impossibility.

So like Nicodemus and all of us humans, to get that that place Jesus is talking about, all you have to do is ask Jesus to come into your life and be Lord over your soul. Give your life to Jesus and he will one day welcome both you, me and all that believe on that name. He will say, " well done my good and faithful servant, well done." Now enter into my rest! Amen Saints!

62
SIMPLE TRUTH

In the beginning was the Word, and the Word was with God, and the Word was God.
John 1:1

The word is what brought all of this forward. Thou word shall I sew(place, bind, hold dear, rely on) in my heart, that I might not sin against God. This is the infallible truth that he made us and not we ourselves. The theory of evolution cannot explain away that God, Jesus and the Holy Spirit is the only rational truth of evidence of man's origin and this created world. Evolution is just science fiction but the Word is the absolute truth of the existence of a pre-existent God.

When you examine the words, in the beginning. What does that thought bring to your natural mind. The start of something? True. So if you believe that from a natural premise, then you have to rationally believe that there was something before to initiate that beginning. Man has always tried to figure out things and explain them so that he appeared as the absolute authority. Man's intelligence comes by way of the supreme authoritative sovereignty of our Almighty God.

If God did not will for man to understand some of his nature, we would be as lost as the children of Israel trying to get to the promise land without the guidance of God. So in determining your future, you have to acknowledge where your beginning comes from. Imagine a world which has no beginning or starting point of origin?

When thinking about the beginning, to understand it, really you have to be in the spirit, because the natural will leave you with unanswered questions. And in reality, you have to take God at his word to make it, and still there are things about him, we will never come to know, because there is so much to him that is too much for us to understand. He does give us enough truths about himself for us to accept him and believe on his Holy name. Amen Saints! Have a blessed day.

63
ETERNAL REWARDS

But as it is written, Eye hath not seen, nor ear heard, neither have entered into the heart of man, the things which God hath prepared for them that love him. **1 Corinthians 2:9**

That thing that God has prepared for you in the heavenly realm will not be realized until that day. This realization will be with your heavenly mind realizing the God that promised you that in that day you will see him just as he is. The building he talks about that is not made by man's hand is one of the things that is unimaginable to our human intellect.

One of the things that we do know is that Jesus is real and he went back to the Father to prepare a place for his children that his ultimate plan is for us to live in peace, harmony and unspeakable joy in that prepared place for all of his prepared children. The prepared children are all who have accepted Christ as their personal Lord and Savior.

There are things known and things unknown which are not knowable until our arrival inside heavens gates. God gives us the opportunity to experience things here on earth which are a precursor to the unrealized splendor of heaven, that will only be revealed at the appointed time.

So in the meantime, accept what he has for us here and wait in great anticipation for your rewards of heavens destiny for us as believers. Now this preparation for us by God is only for those that love him. Accepting him is actually loving him which is a requirement but it is a volitional choice. Amen Saints! Have a blessed night.

64
NOT GUILTY

Saying, Blessed are they whose iniquities are forgiven, and whose sins are covered.
Romans 4:7

Only the blood of Christ can cleanse us of this. Disobedience is just walking opposite the will of God and having not asked for forgiveness through Jesus Christ our Lord. The joy, happiness or blessedness comes through the salvation offered from the Father through the Son Jesus.

There is no other way or method we can truly be protected and our Salvation secured other than the door that Christ offers. Many times we want to forget some things that have happened or is currently happening in our lives. Coming to Christ offers the refreshing forgiving waters where our sins of disobedience are placed by Christ, never to be brought up again.

Many times for the believer, the problem is that Christ

has forgotten our trespasses but the devil won't let you forget. Sometimes it's us not letting go of the past. Because of our past, the enemy is the only one bringing it up again and we have to realize the tricks of the devil. Your past is just that and your best days are ahead of you.

Greater is he that is in me(Holy Spirit) than he(the devil) that's in the world. Believe what the promises are and stop listening to your friends who may not have your best interest at heart. If you want a true friend, one you can always count on, let me recommend my friend who wants to be your friend, Jesus Christ. Allow him in and you will never be the same again. Amen Saints! May the blessings of the Lord be upon you and your families always.

65
HONESTY AND JUSTICE

The just man walketh in his integrity: his children are blessed after him. **Proverbs 20:7**

The motives of the righteous are open and clear for examination. Someone is always watching us for some reason or another. The Lord watches so that he can lead, guide and direct us to all truth. The Justice of God overrules his love.

Our children are watching us and the moves and decisions we make help form their attitudes in life and toward God. You have to live what you tell them, if you tell them that Jesus is the way, you better be living with that same example. Any other way does not reflect the integrity of God.

If your walk in front of your children with the integrity taught to you by God, then more than likely they will walk in the same manner even though they may like you fall off the pathway but they like you will get back on the right track. Why? Because you are walking with your heart in the right place. We have to walk the walk and talk the talk if we claim to have Christian Integrity. Amen Saints!

66
SEARCHING

The name of the Lord is a strong tower: the righteous runneth into it, and is safe.
Proverb 18:10

There does not exist a stronger stronghold than Jesus. Looking for something to carry you through? Need an anchor? How about a solid rock? How about a guiding light in a secret storm you may be going through? In your search for tomorrow, what are you doing about today?

There is but one answer for all of these questions. His name is Jesus Christ our Lord. Who is your anchor, your guiding light, your rock, your stronghold? Many people find their answer in the wrong thing or things. These things can become problematic in our lives. What do you mean you might ask? The temporary fixes in the issues of life that we come across are just that temporary. The have no long term value.

On the other hand, the word and promises of God are designed to serve as the lighthouse that shines distinctive enough for you to be led straight to him who is your stronghold and your salvation and your strength, an ever present help when we run into the wrong types of strongholds. If you need protection, then he is all that you need and all he ask in return for his help is our obedience.

God's word is all the relevance we need for yesterday, today and tomorrow. The Lord says"I am God and I change not." Trust him in the driver's seat and experience where he takes you! It will more than amaze you! It will protect, lead, guide and save you from all hurt, harm and danger.

We place our trust in a lot of people and things who had no part in our creation. Place your trust in the one that created you for his glory and your good while he is recovering you back to himself. We only need recovery when something is lost. Man became lost to the Father when Adam fell in the Garden. Now Jesus was sent to recover God's prized possession. Amen Saints! Have a blessed day and a blessed Sunday Service.

67
WAITING AND TESTING

Beloved, believe not every spirit, but try the spirits whether they are of God: because many false prophets are gone out into the world.
1 John 4:1

Many want you to believe they speak a prophetic word. Just because they say they are praying away this and declaring that. All you have to do is this and on tomorrow or immediately you will receive this blessing or that blessing. Not necessarily judging what they are claiming, but many have ulterior motives of diversions and a quest for filthy lucre.

The scripture says for us to try the spirit by the spirit. What does that mean? Can you find anywhere in the scriptures where Jesus promises that immediately after you pray that this will happen other than the promise of Salvation through the Holy Ghost? Jesus did say that we have to have faith and believe.

Jesus said all things are possible to them that believe. Most times there is a waiting period and a testing or trying of our faith. How can these people who oftentimes are false prophets declare such immediate miracles when Jesus is the only one I know that can speak a word, think it or will it and it happens.

Reliance on the Holy Spirit is our safe way to know from the guidance of The Holy Spirit if the words that these people speak come from God or themselves. Notice that these people say "I declare this and I declare that. What makes you think all of a sudden that what they say comes from God and not from their self indulgence.

Some churches are allowing children to come before the congregations making declarations. Children emulate what they see and hear. There is no I in God nor is their an I in Jesus but there is an I in Salvation and you better get that declaration right.

For many of us our faith, doctrines and beliefs are not rooted in the word but in man and what he promises or declares because of what we see (tangibles, things). The gospel of Jesus is not defined in declarations but in acts of faith and obedience. Amen Saints! Have a blessed day.

68
CARRYING OUR BURDENS

Bear ye one another's burdens, and so fulfil the law of Christ. **Galatians 6:2**

Christ will carry for us all that we can't. In times like these where the enemy tries to zap our strength and courage with his displays of trying to inflict fear in us, Christ the solid rock is our anchor. He didn't give us a spirit of fear or timidity but a spirit of love and a sound mind. All of us at one time of another have had our faith challenged by the onslaught of the enemy.

Greater is he that is in me(Christ) than he(the devil) that is in the world. The faith world of the believer enjoins us to help one another when we are troubled by the issues we go through whether real or imagined. This can happen when we focus on the world rather than Christ and his promises.

Stand up and stand on the promises of God and turn them over to him and rest(trust him) he will take care of it. Rest assured that his promises will be fulfilled. Going through something or is the enemy trying to rattle you like he often tries? Run to the Rock and he will take care of you. Whatever the problem is, I can always go to the rock(Jesus Christ our Lord). I am my brothers keeper.

The scripture says that we who are believers should help shoulder the troubles of our fellow believers, which fulfills the laws of Christ. That means we are following the commands of Christ and in so doing, we are blessed for it. Amen Saints! Have a wonderfully blessed day and weekend and a most blessed Sunday.

69
FLESH

Every way of a man is right in his own eyes: but the Lord pondereth the hearts. **Proverbs 21:2**

Our own thoughts is what gets us oftentimes into entanglements. When it comes to our own conclusive thoughts, we really believe we are right. Our rationalization makes us feel sure about our conclusions we come to. Our decisions are based on what we feel are in our best interest. We feel sure that there is no way that we can be wrong in the slightest.

We speak with self assurance that we are right and everybody else is wrong. The slightest intimation from someone else's opinion can let loose a reservoir of furor from us. You don't know what I have been through, you don't know what they have done me, is what we say or feel about the matter.

Job's three friends had that same attitude toward Job when

he was being tested by the devil from the authority given him from God. His friends didn't know as well as Job, what God had allowed the devil to do and the constraints placed on the devil by God in relationship to Job's soul.

We as well as our friends can get it wrong if we make these declarations out of our natural minds instead of accepting the guidance of the Holy Spirit. Now we can be right sometimes but God is always right and his judgements are just and fair. He looks at our hearts and doesn't look at or hold us to what comes out of our mouths. If God judged us from what we say, then we would probably be in a bad state of being.

Watch your mouth and let the Holy Spirit lead you to the safe shores. Don't let your ego lead you down the wrong pathway. Self pride can keep you from the blessings that God has already ordered for you that is held in escrow until it's time to access them according to your obedience in time(where you are in this world). Amen Have a wonderfully blessed day.

70
PATIENCE AND TOLERANCE

Be ye angry, and sin not: let not the sun go down upon your wrath. **Ephesians 4:26**

Remember to proceed with caution and act according to the spirit. In our world today there are so many things that are designed to give rise to our temperament. The car that cuts you off, the person at the supermarket that sees you about to turn into the parking space but cuts in and parks and just get out of the car and walks off like they didn't see you. The neighbor that allows their pets the use your lawn as their restroom after you have ask them repeatedly to control their pet. Annoying phone calls after you have asked to be put on a do not call list. Things going on in the church that have no spiritual value.

What Jesus saw going on in the temple is what caused to be moved with righteous indignation. They were price gauging, gambling and taking advantage of people in the house of prayer. When Jesus recognized what they were doing, he immediately began to correct the situation and told them, "this is a house of prayer but you have made it a den of thieves." He began to turn over tables and ran them out. Notice he corrected the situation, told them what wrong they were doing, reminded them where they were and the purpose for the place and did not sin in doing so.

When we follow God's plan in correction According to the word, it works out to his glory and his praise and not our plan but his. The issues of life are sometimes not easy to handle but God has already mapped out a way for us that is decent and in order and its design is to help the wrongdoer recognize his ways and to bless heaven with our actions.

Now the take away from this scripture is that no matter how you have been wronged or offended, we should be reconciled and not go to sleep angry with person that has caused the offensive actions toward you. Someone has to take the high road, even when you are not wrong. Jesus did just that when he died on the cross in payment for what sins you and I and this world had committed.

He looked beyond our faults and saw and solved our needs. Remember, while we were yet in our sins, Christ died for the ungodly (humanity). So you can correct something or someone that is wrong, but don't do so with worldly solutions, put on Christ. Amen Saints! Have a blessed day.

71
WORSHIP AT CHURCH

For where two or three are gathered together in my name, there am I in the midst of them.
Matthew 18:20

Forsake not the assembly of the believers. There is power when the people of God get together at the hour of prayer which is the church. I am speaking of the physical building where the word of God is released, taught or spoken. Before there was TBN, 700 Club and many of the televangelist programs we see or take part in today. The only way we received the word of God in worship was by attending the local churches in our communities.

It was important then and still should be now for the family to attend a local church service in our community. Our blessings come in part from our obedience in the act of attending and our participation in church service. Our praise through this type of worship is essential. Television church attendance is alright if you have some ailment that prevents you from being able to physically go to the church.

But many times we have become somewhat lazy about church attendance. The blessing is in being in the house of prayer and being in the midst of God and other believers. Times today are perceived differently than in Old Testament days when you had to go to the place of worship and bring something of offerings so that the Levite Priests could make atonement for your sins. Now because we are in the church age and we are saved by grace through faith we have become lackadaisical.

God still wants us to come to the place where he and his people assemble and bring his gifts and praise him together. He said where two or three gather together in his name, he would be there with them. There are blessings when you go to church that you don't get when you stay at home watching church on tv. There wasn't tv's in Moses, the prophets and Jesus day, you had to go and meet for the blessings. Make it a practice or habit to go meet Jesus at his house. Amen Saints! Have a blessed day.

72
U-TURNS ALLOWED

I the Lord search the heart, I try the reins, even to give every man according to his ways, and according to the fruit of his doings.

Jeremiah 17:10

What are you challenged by or in search of? The heart or our deeds can be from a dark place and an evil and desperately wicked origin. The Lord is the only one who really knows exactly what is going on in our lives. Some of us are very cunning, smooth, evasive, slick, deceptive and shocking. The truth about the matter is that the flesh coupled with the heart can cause us and others undeserved misery and harm.

That's why it is imperative for us to not yield to the pressures of the flesh. We are responsible for our thoughts and ultimately our actions. We may not see or know what's in each other's thoughts and minds. The Lord is the one who examines our hearts, thoughts and motives. They are transparent to God and we know exactly our intents.

The word, which he is, is sharper than a two edged sword and it had the power and intelligence to determine and know precisely the heart and intents of a man (his creation). We will receive from our own actions, what we justly deserve from what God determines that should be. The good news is that because of his unfailing love he is willing to forgive us and keep us from the snares of the enemy.

Christ paid for our freedom but we have to choose to make the u turn, repent and come back to him, our arc of safety. There are many assurances of his promises of restoration in the scriptures (The Holy Bible). All we need to do is access them and sincerely apply them and he will help us rise above our troubles.

We really get better than we deserve many times. We deserved death because of our sin but Christ stepped in and died for us with his life, so a turn around by us should be in order. Amen Saints! Have a wonderfully blessed day.

73
STRADDLING THE FENCE

For to be carnally minded is death; but to be spiritually minded is life and peace.

Because the carnal mind is enmity against God: for it is not subject to the law of God, neither indeed can be.

So then they that are in the flesh cannot please God. **Romans 8:6-8**

The flesh creates a gulf between us and God. The flesh left unchecked causes us to stay on the road that leads to death and destruction. In the flesh are stagnant waters that should not be consumed.

Carnality is a baby Christian who is back and forth between two opinions, what God says and what the world says. In other words, a carnal mind (the world) causes one to have issues between that person and God. The spiritual mind renders understanding of spiritual matters and our responsibility to the Father. It allows us to have peace with God. Or carnal mind does not recognize nor respect God's law. So in the flesh we cannot please God. Amen Saints.

74
THE LIGHT AND THE WAY

For every one that doeth evil hateth the light, neither cometh to the light, lest his deeds should be reproved.

But he that doeth truth cometh to the light, that his deeds may be made manifest, that they are wrought in God. **John 3:20-21**

His light shows us and leads us to him. Jesus says "I am the way the truth and the life, no man can come to the Father but by me the Son." These words are tried and true and is the only way we can reconcile ourselves to The Father. I read a most disturbing post that basically said that what we read in the Scripture are just stories. They are not infallible truths and there is in essence no God.

They went on to say that we are our own gods. How tragic for this person if he doesn't ever learn and accept the truth. So the rich man in hell and his looking up to heaven and seeing Lazarus is just a story and not one of God's infallible truths? One man believes in the Quran and another in Buddha, but the fact is that these two men are still dead and buried in a grave and our Lord has risen and is back in his rightful place, seated at the right of his and our Father.

Now, whose report do you believe? God or man. Joshua said" As for me and my house, we will serve the Lord." Now with that, all that are in his household will be saved,sealed, sanctified and will enter into eternal salvation with Christ Jesus according to their faith. The takeaway is that we have to believe, trust and have faith in the only one true and living God. His name is Jesus and he reigns from heaven above, with power and Dominion Authority.

When we trust, We gladly come to the light and evil is not present with us, for we know that the light sees straight through darkness and our evil is revealed.But the redeemed don't mind coming to the light because we know that he can see what we are doing and what our plans are.

Our thoughts and plans are okay with God because they are alive in Christ. Be alive and come to the light because he is our strength and our way to eternal reward there and our assurance here on earth that he will provide for us. Amen Saints! I thank God for these 44 years of marriage today! What a blessing!

75
DESTINY

But whoso keepeth his word, in him verily is the love of God perfected: hereby know we that we are in him.

He that saith he abideth in him ought himself also so to walk, even as he walked.

1 John 2:5-6

Execution or Execution, they both leads us to that place of eternal destination. When we follow Christ our actions lead us to that place where his grace and mercy comes from. When we follow our own righteousness and never confess Christ, we then end up in the other place of eternal destiny in hell forever.

The actions in our lives can only come from one of two places, heaven or hell and we are responsible or the cause for it. Execution is just an action but we are the ones who put it into action. When we keep the word of God active in our lives, it keeps us out of harm's way and we remain in fellowship and alive, active, secured and refuged in him.

When the believer says he is abided in him, we ought to walk, live, breathe and trust just as Christ did while here on earth and then we shall be welcomed home in heaven one day. Our Salvation secures our place in heaven one day, but we should live here on earth to his glory and his praise by wholesome living and wholesome thoughts.

Our daily walk says who and what is controlling and influencing us. His love is made perfect in us when we fall and use the rebound technique of 1 John 1:9. Repent of your sins against heaven, let Christ cleans us up and move on. Don't let the enemy say we are dirty when Christ says you are clean, wash by the blood of the lamb. Amen Saints! Have a blessed day in the Lord.

76
HEAVEN'S FIX

A father of the fatherless, and a judge of the widows, is God in his holy habitation.

Psalm 68:5

He is a defender of those with no defense. A father to the fatherless, a mother to the motherless, a friend to the friendless and hope for the hopeless is our God. Our God says, " I am whatever you need me to be to you and for you I am." He reigns from heaven above with sovereign power and authority.

This scripture declares that he does this from his holy dwelling place which is not in the corrupted world that we temporarily live in. All hope is not lost if your hope is the risen Christ. Our focus should be on things above, even though we live down here below. When focus on above, he fixes what needs to be fixed here below for you. When we face our problems, he fixes them one by one and not all at once.

You didn't get all of your difficulties at once so don't expect them to be fixed all at once, even though he could if he willed it so. How can you gain confidence and experience if there is no test or waiting period which we gain faith and perseverance that yields patience. He told his disciples to wait and all who become witnesses and disciples will have to wait on his promises and the onslaught of his eminent power. Amen Saints! Happy Father's Day everyone. Have a blessed day with the family. He willed it so.

77
GIVING AND BLESSINGS

Which was the son of Enos, which was the son of Seth, which was the son of Adam, which was the son of God. **Luke 3:38**

Give and it will given unto you, bless others and you will be blessed also. The Lord told Abraham " I will bless them that bless you and I will curse them that curse you." It is blessing to be a blessing. God will bless those who have a heart to bless others and those whose motive to give is not born out of receiving something in exchange.

Now the scripture tells us that when our giving is driven by spiritual obedience to the word, that's where the return of overflow comes in. When we give without the expectation of receiving, that opens the windows of God's blessings from his throne room. The good measure, pressed down, shaken together and running over is God's way of letting us know, that he blesses us well pass what we are able to give him. This is our test from God in obedience.

Many people fail this test because we give to God after we pay our expenses and many times we even delay paying our expenses. We use the excuse that I can't give God first because I will fall short of money. You are right in the falling short aspect, because when we don't give him the first fruit of our increase on what we receive, he can't give us the promise of what this scripture declares.

When we give back to God off the top of our increase, that's when he causes men to give to you. This giving by man to you comes by way of him from his throne room. So this giving from your heart to God by obedience is returned to you from his heart, with much more than you gave, which allows for you to more than meet your obligations.

From your 100%, he only wants 10%, and now he wants to see how you manage the 90% he left you with, plus the extra gains he sends you because of your obedience in your giving to his storehouse according to Mal. 3:8. We will be blessed if we begin to follow God's plan instead of ours. It all belongs to him anyway. Amen Saints! Happy Father's Day!

78
OUR DEFENDER AND OUR DEFENSE

For we wrestle not against flesh and blood, but against principalities, against powers, against the rulers of the darkness of this world, against spiritual wickedness in high places.
Ephesians 6:12

In spiritual warfare, you cannot see who or what you are fighting with. Only God has the power to see who and what we are fighting and the place or places of its origin. It appears that we are in a losing battle since we cannot see, feel or touch our adversary the devil. That's what the Lord is saying in that this battle belongs to the Lord.

He knows The Who, where, when and what of the wicked and his plots. Many times we can't see what's lurking in the high and dark places but God can see right through all things, high, low and things that are hidden from us. We are not in a fair fight, because are not fighting against flesh and blood or a human adversary that is out in the pen that we can.

This enemy is a spiritual darkness and the vilest of the worst kind. Vial, meaning something that means to do us harm. This is a cosmic enemy, one who has the power to disguise himself. Another admonishment from God is that we put on the whole armor of God because of whom we are wrestling with.

The enemy has the audacity to fight and challenge God. Now if he doesn't respect God, what do you think he wouldn't do to you. God is our protector and we should let him handle this kind of foe. Those that fight against God's people are really fighting against God himself. Just know this, the enemy (the devil) can't win.

We might not know where he is and we might can't see him, but God sees and knows just where he is. Evil can only be dispelled and revealed by light, which comes from God. When the light shines on darkness, it cannot stay in the presence of light. Run to the light and be saved. Amen Saints! Have a blessed day and a wonderful Father's Day to our fathers.

79
THE RACE AND THE REWARD

Let your light so shine before men, that they may see your good works, and glorify your Father which is in heaven. **Matthew 5:16**

What is your life projecting in the sight of God and others? As we run this race of life, what can be said about the way we live and how we treat others. Do we interpose our own desires or do we reflect the qualities and character traits of our Heavenly Father? Light illuminates directly in the spot or area of its beam.

Our light is our life and it is lit up so that we as well as others can see what qualities and deeds we let off. The farther away we allow ourselves to get from the light which is Christ, the dimmer our way is and consequently we lose our way. The closer we are to the light of Christ, the better we can see our way because he is directing our steps and lighting up our pathways.

Sometimes we run into trouble for a number of reasons,

mainly because we choose the wrong entry. The right way is toward the narrow gate that few find, but all that want to find it will find it, because of its distinctive illumination of it heavenly glow of the father's light of love and refuge. The broadway has a light also, but its is the broadway whose pathway leads to doom and destruction.

The Broadway's light is not really light but like the appearance of water in the desert that is only a mirage. A mirage is not useful but he light of God leads to eternal life and everlasting peace. It's our choice to choose God's light of life or the mirage of the devil that leads to eternal damnation. Light or mirage, you make the call. Amen Saints! Have a blessed day.

80
AGAPE OR UNCONDITIONAL LOVE

If a man say, I love God, and hateth his brother, he is a liar: for he that loveth not his brother whom he hath seen, how can he love God whom he hath not seen? **1 John 4:20**

The question of love from God's perspective. How can you love something that you have not seen and not have love for the things you do see. This is what this scripture is alluding to. The action of love that we have for one another is evidenced by a spiritual connection. We see one another but many times just don't have that love for each other, no matter what we may do for one another.

It may be what the bible calls a conditional love based on what we do for one another. So when we can no longer do for one another, we sometimes no longer have love. True love is unconditional and it persist regardless to whether or not i can do or not do for the people in our lives. Whoever says that they love God yet has hate or enmity toward his brother or sister is a liar because it is inconsistent with the definition of what God's love is which is unconditional or agape love.

When we cannot love our brother or sister according to the word, we fall short of really loving God because his will is for us to love one another. This was the new commandment her said I bring to you" That you love one another regardless of your relationship with one another.

Love is the basic fundamental characteristic of God's character. Now when we can love one another unconditionally, then God says only then can you truly love me, even though you have not seen me whether physical or as a spirit. Loving those that you see is evidence that establishes your love for whom you cannot see yet. Yet in a little while you will see me. Amen Saints! Have a blessed day and week.

81
THE CHARACTER OF LOVE

Love worketh no ill to his neighbour: therefore love is the fulfilling of the law. **Romans 13:10**

Love keeps no record! Love beareth and upholdeth all things. Love is patient. Love is kind. Husbands love your wives as I have loved the church and given myself as a ransom for many. Wives submit to your own husbands. Submission is an offspring of love. God is love but his Justice overrules his love.

Love thy neighbor as thyself. Jesus said" I give yo you a new commandment that your love one another." Now since Christ loved us enough to lay down his life, why is it so difficult for us the love our fellow brothers and sisters in the way Christ commanded us to do? Love is an action word that compels us to show our love rather than talk about it and never put it into action.

When you look at love from man's perspective, we might say how difficult it is to love someone who has done so much wrong to you. Then we have to take in account the love that Jesus showed not talked about. From a human viewpoint, you may come to the conclusion that, I wouldn't have done it if I had to make the same decision. That's why he is God. He looked beyond our faults and saw our needs.

Do you have the capacity to look beyond their faults and minister to their needs? In the spirit of Christ you can but not in your flesh. Love overcomes a multitude of faults. Love does not allow you to mistreat or do harm to your neighbor. When Jesus told him to love his neighbor, he asked Jesus"Who is my neighbor?" Your neighbor is anyone who may be in need of your help.

A kind word, a hug, you telling them about Jesus and his saving grace and many other things available in his kingdom for the benefit of his children. Love fulfills and it does not destroy and it keeps no record of what it does. Only God keeps the record of our lives here in earth for recall when we stand before him and give an accurate account. Amen Saints! . Have a lovely day today and always.

82
INFLUENCES

Righteousness keepeth him that is upright in the way: but wickedness overthroweth the sinner. **Proverbs 13:6**

When we follow the path of righteousness we find ourselves unwilling to do anyone intentional harm. There are many times when the enemy seeks to sift us as wheat. He recalls all of the times in our memory when we felt we have been wronged and we automatically want to lash out at someone.

This is an old trick used by the enemy to keep us out of fellowship with Christ. When the enemy succeeds at his evil plan to keep us unbalanced, we are no good for service of kingdom business. When we are in fellowship, we realize what the enemy is doing, so we apply the principle of rebuke and bind.

When we apply the scriptures that we stand on, the enemy can't win. We are blameless by the blood of Christ and it directs the pathways that we should travel. When we are controlled and influenced by sin, we see the only out as being led by evil influences which come from hell. People's nature is basically good because we got our start from the creator. Somewhere from our start and where we find ourselves today, for many of us we have bought into the worlds folly.

We can pray about sin, but we have to be taught out of evil. If sin has its grip on you, come back to Christ or accept him as your Lord and Master and view this world from a whole new spiritual perspective. God is and always will be the answer to everything seen and unseen. Amen Saints!

83
HYPOCRISY

Wherefore the Lord said, Forasmuch as this people draw near me with their mouth, and with their lips do honour me, but have removed their heart far from me, and their fear toward me is taught by the precept of men: **Isaiah 29:13**

I hear your words but your heart is far from me! Many people try and flatter you with pretty words and phony actions. We can be fooled by this many times until the spirit reveals to us what is really going on. The young man says"I will take care of your daughter for the rest of our lives, only she finds him to be abusive and non attentive."

If you give me that position, I will do this nation proud, only to find after the fact his real agenda of self grandiosity. God if you get me out of this one, I will not do this anymore and I will serve you more, only to find ourselves walking away from what we promised God we would do. God knows our hearts, thoughts and minds before they are formed in us.

We can't fool God, he knew what Adam and Eve were going to do before he made both of them and placed Adam first in the garden and gave him the rules. When we apply more of man's teachings rather than God's, we dishonor God and bring shame to ourselves and his kingdom.

The good news is that we can change the direction of our hearts through Salvation in Jesus Christ and walking circumspectly before him. I am not talking perfectly but as rightly as we can by the power of The Holy Spirit. He will help you help yourself by the guidance of his spirit. We are saved by his grace through faith and kept by his mercy and the blood of his son Jesus Christ. Amen Saints! Have a wonderfully blessed day today.

84

I AM

For I am persuaded, that neither death, nor life, nor angels, nor principalities, nor powers, nor things present, nor things to come

Romans 8:38

The Great I Am controls our mountains and he calms the turbulent seas of life. When Moses was commissioned by God to lead and speak to Israel, Moses had no confidence in his own abilities. He told God about an imperfection in his speech, as if God did not know this already. He was talking to God but he still asked God " Who shall I say sent me?" God said" Tell them that I Am sent you."

Now I Am is Supremely Sovereign over all and made all things seen and unseen. The question is, are you available for your assignments? God gives us the ability to do the work by his sovereign power and authority. He just wants us to avail ourselves for the work in his vineyard. That's all he wanted from Moses and that's all he wants from us.

God spoke from the Mountain of Sinai which is a place of victory. Our mountains represent the troubles we experience along life's journey. The God that spoke from that mountain and gave Moses the Laws of God is the same God that will ultimately conquer our mountains and our seas of conflict in our lives. Another time when the name I Am came up was when someone spoke of Abraham and the Lord said" Before Abraham was I Am." Nothing is greater or existed before or after God.

In this picture, there is a light that is leading to the mountains and a light that is above the mountains which should tell us that God is that light and he controls the mountain. Our victories over our troubles can only come through God, Jesus and The Holy Spirit. What we are led to and what we are delivered from comes from the hand and blessings of God.

The same God that opened the Red Sea for Israel to cross over their trouble is the same God that will allow for your safe passage over your Red Sea of trouble. We conquer only through the our love and obedience to the great I Am, Jesus Christ our LORD. When you miss the formula, you miss the blessings. Jesus is the only way out and up. Amen Saints! Have a remarkably wonderful and blessed day.

85
THE BLOOD

But I say unto you which hear, Love your enemies, do good to them which hate you,

Bless them that curse you, and pray for them which despitefully use you. **Luke 6:27-28**

Those that hear the voice of Christ and follow his commands belong to the church. The church is not the physical building we worship in. It's the Holy Spirit that dwells within us. The Holy Spirit allows us to hear and act according to the voice that gave us the spirit from the Son of God.

Jesus said"My sheep know my voice and no other voice will they follow." Christ is saying, listen to me those of you who understand and acknowledge what I am saying to you. Love not hate them that do you wrong, it's hard but I say love them, many will hate you, you realize that many hated me but I did not curse them, in fact those that persecuted me, I asked my father to forgive because that really did know to whom or what they were really doing.

So in like manner for you being my child, pray for them especially those who really intentionally try to do you harm and go about their days plotting against you. I know what they are doing and I can see everything. Our job is to love and do Good toward them, it is the will of God to do so. God the great equalizer will straighten things out. Remember we were once enemies of God, but by his grace, we were reconciled to him by his blood.

So if God through the Son could do for us what he did for us in spite of us, we can also do the same toward our enemies, only through the power of The Holy Spirit. Now we can only understand this and have the will to do this by his power and not ours. Now let us praise him for the power he gives us to overcome through his spirit. Amen Saints!

86
FEAR AND REST

There is no fear in love; but perfect love casteth out fear: because fear hath torment. He that feareth is not made perfect in love.

1 John 4:18

Fear is a respect for the authority of God and the beginning of Spiritual wisdom. The enemy sends his idea of fear on the world in many different forms and fashions. His fear is simply (False Evidence Appearing Real).

The enemy tries to keep our minds focused on the torments he keeps in rapid fires of his hurling false accusations against us. This scripture says there is no fear in love. This is true because God is love and he cast out or off the troubles of this world that incites that kind of mindset.

The fear that God wants us to realize is that his fear initiates our respect for his Divine authority and respect for his character. When we realize that his nature is for us to come to know his will by our inquiries of what we need to do to make it in this world and the eternal world hereafter.

So our interest and that of God is best served with the knowledge of whom shall I fear? God or man? Following the leadership of God leads us to a place of peace and rest. Do you want peace and rest? Then fear God and rest in the cradle of his love and eternal promises. Amen Saints! Have a blessed day and week.

87
CARES

Casting all your care upon him; for he careth for you. **1 Peter 5:7**

Give all your concerns, troubles, worries and the unrest the enemy tries to bother you with , to God who is able to protect you. When the fisherman cast or launches his line into to water, his expectation is to catch a fish. When the believer cast his concerns in the refreshing and healing waters of God, he expects to get an answer to his delima or his condition.

God is the only person that has a truly genuine and an unconditional care for you and me. God is simply saying to us, bring every one of your troubles to me so I can solve and rescue you from your troubles. Our solutions are only temporary. When we problem solve, our troubles come right back up. When Christ intervenes for us as our intercessor with the Father, our troubles are permanently solved and we should move forward and not look back.

When we look back most times, it's the enemy trying to pull you back into what God has already pulled you out of. It doesn't matter how many cares you have, God says cast or leave all of them with him. Give them all to him and continue to walk in his light and let him cast off the darkness that the enemy tries to cast over you.

The Apostle Paul says "I've learned to be content in whatever condition or circumstance I found myself in, but he didn't mean for us to stay still as a result, but to keep moving forward with the help of Christ that gave us the guidance of the Holy Spirit. Amen Saints! Have a blessed and wonderful Memorial Day.

88
DO NOT MIX

Wherewithal shall a young man cleanse his way? by taking heed thereto according to thy word. **Psalm 119:9**

Fresh as the morning dew are the daily blessings of God. How can God's creations pathways remain refreshed, clean and safe to travel on? The scripture declares" by listening to and following the guidance and instructions of the word. Directions are to be followed and maintained for the safety of the reader.

The notice says" caution, may cause electrical shock." If you mix water and electricity together, you will have a problem, the two are not ment to be mixed. Just like, grace and evil, the two don't fare well together. That's why the Lord says " choose you this day whom you will serve or whom you will allow to control you.

Notice the word "will", it is our choice. God is good and the devil is evil. He makes it plain, their is no trick to this statement, you choose and the reward is plain. Christ means eternal rewards in heaven and the devil means an eternal reward in hell. We make the call. Who and what is your choice? Let me give you some help on this one. Make Jesus your choice today if you haven't already.

Their is no trick in Jesus, but their is triumph. Jesus wants you, the question is, do you want him? Power, deliverance and everything you need is in him. Give Jesus a chance and you will never be the same again. That's an assurance from the word of God. He is on the main line, tell him what you need. Amen Saints! The blessings of the Lord be upon you.

89
SOVEREIGNTY AND PROVIDENCE

The Lord bless thee, and keep thee:

The Lord make his face shine upon thee, and be gracious unto thee:

The Lord lift up his countenance upon thee, and give thee peace. **Numbers 6:24-26**

It's the Lords business as to how we fare in this life and the great hereafter. It's our choice as to whether or not we accept the business he wills for us. The business I am speaking of is his providence, his sovereignty, his deity and his supreme authority. His plans for us are in part unknown but he has given us enough knowledge of his plan through his son and the written word.

He is the keeper and the one who blesses our lives and causes his light to shine upon us. His light shines on all who know and trust him and that's how he is aware of where we are and and keeps us out of harm's way. His armor keeps us safe that's why he encourages us to put on the whole armor of God and keep it on.

We don't know when the devil is going to attack. We are vulnerable without the protection of this armor. When the Lord causes his face to shine upon us, he is lighting our pathways so that we might see our way and that is his grace being spread upon us.

The Lord places his spirit upon us through the blood of Jesus and that is the peace we experience in our lives daily until he receives us in glory to give him praise eternally forever. Amen Saints! Have a wonderfully blessed day.

90
HAPPINESS

Delight thyself also in the Lord: and he shall give thee the desires of thine heart.

Psalm 37:4

There are many things we can find enjoyment in. But there is only one thing or mainstay we can experience true joy, happiness, peace and contentment. This can only be found in God The Father, God The Son and God The Holy Spirit. When we focus on doing the will of God and serving his people, only then does the Lord find us operating inside of his will.

When we ask for things inside of the will of God, he permits us to receive what we want, because he knows then that we can handle it. Often times our desires don't coincide with his will, that's why many people make the statement "I have been praying to God for a long time for some things, but he hasn't answered me yet." That's because what we are praying for and asking isn't in his will yet or it may never be.

Ask yourself these questions. Is what I am asking God good for his kingdom? Will it bring praise to his name? Will it honor him or me? Will it help others as well as me? Am I spiritually mature enough to handle it? When what we ask for blesses his name, his people and is an unselfish request, that's when he gives us what we ask for at the appropriate time. All request are time oriented according to his blessing calendar. He will eventually answer us, we just have to be patient and wait. Amen Saints!

91
THE PRIZE

Delight thyself also in the Lord: and he shall give thee the desires of thine heart.

Acts 20:24

Now we must allow ourselves to run this race with patience and endurance. We that have have chosen Christ, have chosen a good work. This race as we run it will have others in the race running for the same prize. The good news is that all who have chosen to run will be crowned with the prize by the righteous Judge, our Lord and Savior Jesus Christ.

The prize is goodness and mercy, guidance and protection as we run on the tracks of life. Sometimes on the tracks, obstacles get in the way, but Jesus assures us that he has overcome the world and its obstacles. It does not mean that we will not have them but we are assured by the blood of Christ that through Jesus we will overcome them by the power of the Holy Spirit.

In this life the ultimate mission is to complete the work as best we can that the Lord has given us to do. Our aim and our goal and mission is to not let the enemy discourage us or stop us from keeping focus on the plan that God has for us to succeed by what the Apostle Paul said " I have fought a good fight, kept the faith and finished my course. and now there is laid up for me a crown, that the righteous Judge will give me in that day." Keep running, keep the faith, have patience and stand on the promises and surely you will win the prize. Success here in the earth and heaven when we get home. Amen Saints!

92
THE CHALLENGES

Now faith is the substance of things hoped for, the evidence of things not seen. **Hebrews 11:1**

Through Faith we receive what we actually need and not necessarily what we ask for. The ridges or obstacles or challenges of life are very confusing in relationship to faith. We know as believers that God will make a way for us somehow. In the myriad of all that life sometimes throw our way, we can lose sight of who controls our world and our destiny.

The scripture declares" The earth is the Lords and the fullness thereof and they that dwell there in. The Lord has not relinquished anything to the enemy that he is not in control of. The enemy is controlled by the power of God which he allows him to place us into testing so that our faith can grow toward him (Jesus). Sometimes God has to shake us up before we can be shaped up according to his image.

This because we hear but don't listen. Listening is an action word that causes us to make a decision on what we are going to do about the situation we find ourselves in. It's like a horse that is brought to a water troft filled with what he needs, which is the water to quench his thirst. Now if the horse recognizes the water and still chooses not to drink and dies because of thirst, whose fault is it?

Like the horse, God is our water of life and he makes that clear throughout the bible. He invites us to accept his living waters but it's left up to us through faith to accept his offer of life and not death. Our faith and trust in God must be strong and our confidence has to such that what we see in the troubles we experience will be overcome by the faith that we believe that we are headed for the green meadows and pastures just beyond the ridges of challenges.

Only faith does this for us and our yielding our lives to the control and influence of the Almighty God. When we get into a storm, don't fret, Jesus is in the storm with us and he controls it, because he is the very eye of the storm, directing it and ultimately bringing it to a halt. Trust God and let him lead you all the way. Finally, mothers, have a happy and blessed Mother's Day. We also remember those mothers that are with the Lord and we thank God for them and all they taught us. Amen Saints!

93
RELATIONSHIP

Mine eyes are ever toward the Lord; for he shall pluck my feet out of the net. **Psalms 25:15**

Just as the beauty of the blooming flower opens, so does the love of God opens up to all that receive him. There are so many distractions in the world, that many are duped by It fascinations. When we focus on the things around us, it leaves little time for us the focus on the only thing that really matters. The only thing that really matters in this life really is our relationship with the Father.

This scripture by the Psalmist focuses itself on the fact that his eyes are always focused on the Lord above. Now he uses the term eyes, but he is really out the fact that his mind and his thoughts are what is focused on the Lord. The word focus here is a deliberate act to be in fellowship with the Lord. When we are looking toward the Lord he is the one who guides our feet in the direction we should go. Have you ever been walking and all of a sudden you began to stumble, because you really didn't see the rise in the sidewalk, and you almost fell and then sometimes you did fall.

Try walking or running and looking down for a few brief minutes, you will eventually run into something. The Psalmist here is saying, when his mind is focused on Jesus, regardless to what calamities that may be going on in your life or around you, God is the one that takes our feet or us out of the traps of the enemy. When we follow the Holy Spirit instead of our old sin nature which is always present and active, we find that we have more ups in this life than downs.

The downs for the believer is really a test or experience that the Lord sends our way to strengthen us. So what the enemy thinks is a trap for us is really what leads ultimately to triumph for a child of God. So as best you can, keep you mind on things above and the Spirit will keep you from the snares of this life most times, except for the test we surely will have to go through, but you won't stay there provided you don't quit.

The Psalmist also declared" When my enemies and my foes came to eat up my flesh (or to destroy me) they stumbled and they fell. " Sing that song of praise" I woke up this morning with my mind, staying on Jesus." Amen Saints!

94
THE WILL

Thy word have I hid in mine heart, that I might not sin against thee. **Psalms 119:11**

Just to follow up on the last portion of this Psalm. This conclusion brings us to another request or benefit. The Psalmist is piggybacking on the request of the hidden word. "That I might not or will not sin against God. The strength that he is requesting is from the power and will of God, not his own fleshly strength.

Man has already shown a weakness in the flesh, starting way back in the Garden with Adam. Paul said" In my flesh dwells no good thing." Every time I try to do good evil is all around." What the Apostle was saying, is that he didn't have the strength from within his flesh to do what was right, so the only way he could do it was from the power found in the spirit that came or comes from God through the Son, Jesus Christ.

He further stated that even the things he knew to do that

was right, he didn't do because of the weakness of his flesh. Also he said, that the very things he knew not to do and didn't want to do, again because of the weakness in his flesh, he did them. The conclusion is that from the request he is believing that, if God keeps his word fresh in our mind, it helps us guard ourselves against sin.

So that's why his request is for God to help him in this way because he knows that he hasn't the power in himself to do what is required in reference to sin. This is the one of the primary reasons God sent Jesus to help us and to live within all who trust him and invite him to be Lord of our lives. But he still leaves the choice up to us. To live or to die, he left the choice up to us. Jesus said" I would that none would perish, but all come into repentance." In short, Jesus is simply saying to us, why not serve me and live? Amen Saints!

95
THE WORD

Thy word have I hid in mine heart, that I might not sin against thee. **Psalms 119:11**

Hidden away for safe keeping and instant recall for immediate use. The Psalmist is asking God to hide his instructions in our innermost memory receptacle. The word hide here means to maintain or to keep in our constant memory this resource for our use when the storms of life come raging in. The only person the word hidden in our heart or mind is hidden from is the devil. God will not hide anything from us that can help us.

What helps us more than the word? Nothing! It's just like his love, nothing can ever separate us from his love! Nothing! So the Spirit stands guard over the things that are hidden from the enemy but are readily recognizable to us and ready for our use. The word is what the Psalmist was referring to.

Who is the Word? God is the Word, so the Psalmist is just

making his request to the Father to maintain himself, hidden in soul from the enemy, but ready for battle when needed. Are you ready for battle? Is the word of God hidden away for you in your arsenal of heavenly promises? Are you rehearsing what the word says so they can be rightly and accurately used.

This request is not like you placing something important somewhere thinking you will remember where you put it. Now when it becomes time for you to use it you, can't remember where it is. No, this time with the word placed in your heart or the mind, when you need it, you know exactly where it is and how to use it for God's Glory. Happy is the man whose trust is in the Lord. Amen Saints!

96
PROMISE

Let us hold fast the profession of our faith without wavering; (for he is faithful that promised;) **Hebrews 10:23**

Don't let the winds of this world blow you off course. The violence and turmoil that the enemy creates is specifically designed by the enemy to keep you fearful and uncertain. The word says that "God did not give us a spirit fear or timidity but a spirit of love, power and a sound mind." The enemy gets us off track when we try and come through our challenges by way of the flesh.

The soul through the Holy Spirit gives us the peace, calm, rational spiritual thinking needed to overcome the wilds of the devil. Cast all your cares on him because he cares for you. That is a scriptural promise when accessed, is one of the most powerfully effective tools you should have in your store house of promise from God. If you don't study, then you don't have any tools or promises to be be placed in your storehouse for future use for yourself or others.

Hebrews 10:23 encourages us to hold on to the trust and assurance of the promise in this scripture. When we hold on to something, no matter how compelling the enemies argument is to let go, don't do it, it is a trap sent from the depths of hell. God will work it out, you may be going through a faith issue and God is weighing out how strong is your faith that you proclaim to have.

God does not play tricks on his children, he leads, guides, protects and ultimately delivers and rescues us from travail. Having issues in this life, which is common to man? Try God's way of survival since your way hasn't worked or has it? Greater is he that is in me than he that is in the world. Our peace is in the spirit and not in the world or flesh. Amen Saints!

97
THE GREAT CHASM CLOSED FOREVER

Neither is there salvation in any other: for there is none other name under heaven given among men, whereby we must be saved. **Acts 4:12**

Jesus said it is finished. That should settle it and also settle you. The question might be asked. Just what did he finish and what does all this entail. The main thing he finished was that he bridged the great gulf of separation between man and God. He tore down the partition so that man could go direct to the Father for what he needed and make his request direct with Jesus as our mediator and intercessor.

He paid the awesome price for man's reproaches. He covered up the enemies lies so that we could hear his voice when we cry Abba Father. He established in our hearts what real and true love is(unconditional). He allowed us to know the difference between straight and crooked. He showed us the way the truth and the life. He closed the finished book with our names sealed in it.

He grafted our souls to the true vine. He gave us to the Father and received us unto himself, that ultimately where he is we shall also be. So by his finishing the work he was sent to do in obedience to the Father, his and ours. We can accept the destiny that God has already provided for us through the finished work of Christ.

The Father sealed our destiny with the blood of his Son Jesus. It happened at Calvary but was spoken from eternity before the world was. Now walk and live in obedience in the knowledge and one day in his presence. Where can I go and his presence is not there? Even if your temple is unclean, he's there also, but he won't dwell or live in you until you let Salvation clean you up through his spirit. Amen Saints!

98
SALVATION

He that believeth on me, as the scripture hath said, out of his belly shall flow rivers of living water. **John 7:38**

While I was yet in my sins, Christ died for the ungodly(you and I). The most important event known to man's assurance of Salvation took place on the place called the skull, Golgotha or Calvary. The place where Jesus died and paid the price for something he didn't do because of his agape love for man.

The barrier that kept a gulf between God and man was brought together by the sacrificial lamb of God. The curtain in the temple was now separated by the blood of Jesus and man could go direct to God himself provided he accepted Jesus as his personal Lord and Savior. The Levite priest no longer had to go before God for man. What Jesus did fixed it then, now and forever. Aren't you glad that the Lord saved you?

He didn't have to do it but he did. As we celebrate Good Friday, The early rising of Christ on that great day on Sunday, the Lord's supper and the seeding of the counselor, the guide called the Holy Spirit is our assurance of God's pleasure in his Sons work on the cross for God's glory and man's good. Let us remember this time and commemorate the living waters that were provided then and still stands today and forever more.

All who believe in this work, the one who did the work sent by him to do this work shall be covered by the blood of the Lamb. When you think about the obedience of the Son and his enduring work and faithfulness to his Father and his love for us, we can't be anything else but thankful. This time is more than Easter eggs, candy and new clothes. But by the grace of God, we are saved, sealed and delivered, looking to the second coming of Christ. Amen Saints!

99
ETERNITY PAST

O taste and see that the Lord is good: blessed is the man that trusteth in him. **Psalms 34:8**

The outcome is awesome. We get more from his blessings than the praise we send up because of the escrow blessings he set up for us long ago. What he did for us in eternity past is blessing us now because of our acceptance of his eternal offer to be a son or daughter of the most high God.

When we are obedient to his will, we then realize what was placed in escrow for us to be received as we mature and pass the test that he sends our way for his praise and our good(maturity). When we look at the word taste, he is simply saying try, experience, take me at my word, trust me, hold on to my promises.

Now the word see means to confirm, validate, witness and give testimony to the evidence in your life what the LORD has, is and will do for his children. We cannot experience the LORD for ourselves with all that he has brought us through and not give personal testimony that he is good. Upon receiving Christ as our personal Lord and Savior, we instantly feel and see through our new spiritual eyes the things we were blinded to when we were in the world.

The last portion of this scripture gives us another benefit of knowing him. It says blessed (happy, covered, chosen, elected, foreknown and predestined. So then we can hide or take cover or refuge in him as a benefit of being a kingdom child. So he is our Father and we can run to him in our distresses and challenges and praise him at the same time because through faith we know he promised to help and deliver us from life's issues and the enemies of the cross. Amen Saints!

100
THE MIND HEART AND SOUL

Keep thy heart with all diligence; for out of it are the issues of life. **Proverbs 4:23**

From out of it flows the issues of life. When we look at the word guard, it simply means to protect at all cost. It means to be up at arms, to have great concern for. When our leaders come and go they have protection from possible attacks on their lives by enemies foreign and domestic.

There is an urgent need to cover them and make sure they stay from what is called imminent danger. Our enemies are always looking for ways to destroy us and to keep us fearful and unhappy. Danger causes us to take certain precautions and travel routes for our safety and well being. Now when it comes to us guarding our heart, no one can do that for us but us. The secret service guards and protects the President, but the Holy Ghost leads, guides and protects the people of God through the indwelling of the Holy Spirit.

The heart is deceitful and desperately wicked. The heart is our think tank and the central system that out of it comes the issues of life . It sets sail to either our conformity or nonconformity to this world and its standards. We and our thinking are transformed or changed by how we are influenced by the spirit of God or our fleshly desires.

The Holy Spirit is the only sure and safe way to guard our thoughts and have a reasonably sure chance at having a safe life's journey. The heart is the mind that determines the course our lives will take. Depending on the heart or your state of mind which can change daily, your life can be up and down, joyful or sad, prosperous or broken, destined for eternity or he'll. We make that choice or call.

That's why the Bible encourages us to guard or protect our mind from the onslaught of the devils attacks through the power and protection of the Holy Spirit. The heart and the Holy Spirit are interrelated and interconnected by volition. Volition is simply a choice we make to follow Christ or the world. Following Christ we find the narrow gate that not many find.

All that believe will find it and the answers to life's problems. Following the world is the broad way that leads to death and destruction and a very tough life here on earth, then there's the pit of hell waiting on you for all eternity. But, you make that decision. Make it easy on yourself, make Jesus your choice. I have decided a long time ago to make Jesus my choice. What about you? If you haven't yet? Do it today! Your decision has eternal ramifications. Amen Saints!

Dr. Garfield E. Como & Judy A. Como

www.ingramcontent.com/pod-product-compliance
Lightning Source LLC
Chambersburg PA
CBHW070533170426
43200CB00011B/2416